THE NURSE IN FAMILY PRACTICE

Practice Nurses and Nurse Practitioners in Primary Health Care

Edited by

ANN BOWLING

and

BARBARA STILWELL

With 10 Contributors

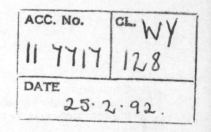
SCUTARI PRESS
London

First published 1988

ISBN 1 871364 13 2

Typeset by Woodfield Graphics, Arundel, West Sussex
Printed and bound in Great Britain by
Biddles Ltd, Guildford and King's Lynn

Contributors

ANN BOWLING BSc MSc PhD, Senior Lecturer, Department of Community Health, London School of Hygiene and Tropical Medicine (University of London), and Department of Community Medicine, City and Hackney Health Authority, London.

BARBARA BURKE-MASTERS RGN RM BSc, Nurse Practitioner, Manna Centre, London.

ANTHONY J CARR RGN NCertDN FHSM FBIM FRCN, Queen's Nurse Management and Nursing Consultant; Former Chief Nursing Officer, Newcastle Health Authority; Member of Review Team on Community Nursing (Cumberlege Committee).

LYNNE CATER BA RGN RM RCNT, Research Assistant, Nursing Studies Unit, University of Nottingham Medical School and Practice Nurse at Two Practices.

GODFREY FOWLER BM FRCGP, General Practitioner, Oxford; Clinical Reader in General Practice, University of Oxford.

ELAINE FULLARD RGN HVCert DipHlthEd, Facilitator of Prevention in Primary Care; Director, Oxford Prevention of Heart Attack and Stroke Project, the Oxford Centre for Prevention in Primary Care, Radcliffe Infirmary, Oxford.

J A MUIR GRAY MD MRCGP FRCP(Glas), Community Physician, Oxfordshire Health Authority, District Department of Community Medicine, Radcliffe Infirmary, Oxford.

PAMELA HAWTHORN PhD RGN RM, Director, Nursing Studies Unit, University of Nottingham Medical School.

DOREEN RESTALL RGN, Nurse Practitioner, Inverurie, Scotland.

BARBARA STILWELL RGN RHV BSc, Researcher, Nurse Practitioner, West Lambeth Health Authority, London.

BARBARA STOCKING BM BA MSc, Director, Health Services Development, King's Fund Centre, London.

PETER TOON MB BS MSc MRCS LRCP MRCGP, Honorary Lecturer, Department of General Practice and Primary Care, St Bartholomew's Hospital, London.

Table of Contents

Preface

It is the aim of the contributors to this book to present recent research findings that document the views and activities of practice nurses in various parts of England, to assess the extent to which the role of the nurse practitioner is a viable development of nursing practice in the UK, and to discuss these topics in the light of past and present political climates. It also attempts to indicate the directions of future developments of the role and outline the essential factors for successful innovation.

Practice nurses are defined here as nurses who are privately employed by general practitioners to work predominantly in the surgery. Nurse practitioners are nurses trained, usually to master's degree level, to perform a range of diagnostic, technical and preventive health care procedures: the role was developed in the USA and, apart from some experiments, is formally undeveloped in the UK.

The varied professional backgrounds of the authors of this volume has inevitably resulted in differences in the presentation of chapters, but we hope that this multidisciplinary approach, which reflects the wide interest in the developing role of practice nurses, has widened its appeal. We feel that the book will be of interest not only to nurse academics, other health care researchers and teachers involved in primary health care but also to policy makers and those involved in care at the grass roots level: the practice nurses, community nurses, nurse managers and general practitioners themselves.

The views expressed in each chapter are those of the individual writers and should not be attributed to the authors collectively.

ANN BOWLING
BARBARA STILWELL
1988

PART I

Conceptual, Practical and Policy Issues

1
The Origins and Development of the Nurse Practitioner Role — a Worldwide Perspective

BARBARA STILWELL

Historical evolution in America

The term 'nurse practitioner' was first used in a demonstration project at the University of Colorado in 1965 (Watson Hawkins & Thibodeau, 1983; Barhydt-Wezenaar, 1981). The project was the brainchild of Dr Henry Silver, a physician, and Dr Loretta Ford, a nurse, who were concerned about the increasing population in the United States and the shortage of primary care physicians. Silver and Ford devised an educational programme for nurses which lasted for four months and included techniques of physical examination:

> '(to prepare) the nurse to furnish comprehensive well child care to children of all ages, to identify and appraise acute and chronic conditions and refer them to other facilities as indicated, and to evaluate and temporarily manage emergency situations until medical assistance is available.'
> (Silver et al, 1967)

The role had had support in the late 1950s from Eugene Stead, a physician at Duke University, North Carolina. He had approached Thelma Inglis, a nurse, and together they devised a master's degree for nurse practitioner training.

Their course was not accredited by the National League of Nursing on the grounds that it meant nurses would be undertaking medical tasks which were felt to be inappropriate and dangerous (Fisher & Horowitz, 1977). Consequently, in

1966 Stead developed the first training programme for physician's assistants at Duke University. Both nurse practitioners and physician's assistants became known as either new health professionals or as physician extenders.

Why did the nurse practitioner role evolve at that time? Sultz et al (1983) stated that it was in response to society's changing health needs. Rogers (1977) commented that it resulted from medicine's inability to deal with simple medical problems. Both these causes were felt to stem from the shortage of physicians in general medical practice: in 1949 64% of physicians were in general practice, but by 1963 the proportion had fallen to 38% and by 1973 to 24%. Raffel (1980) pointed out that the reason for this decline was the lure of specialisation: specialists were paid more and held higher status in society. Similar trends occurred in British general practice resulting in a crisis in manpower in the mid-1960s (Curwen, 1964).

There was also considerable regional variation in the provision of primary care health services in the USA. Rural and inner city areas were unpopular locations for setting up in practice. Rural areas were isolated both socially and professionally, while inner city locations were costly in terms of renting premises: neither area was perceived to be lucrative in a private health care system.

The rising cost of health care was another long standing concern in American society. In 1962, 65% of Americans held private health insurance to cover visits to the general practitioner; by 1977 approximately 75% of the population were privately insured. For those aged 65 years and over without private health insurance there is a federal system, Medicare, which covers home and hospital care. A joint state and federal scheme, Medicaid, provides cover for the poor. The rising costs of health care affected insurance companies and government, as well as consumers who paid increasingly high premiums.

Although these factors gave impetus to the nurse practitioner and physician's assistant movement, both Ford and Silver explain their motives in other terms. Ford's goal was to test an expanded scope of practice for nurses while Silver's concern was to improve child health care (Pearson, 1985). However, it is likely that the government's interest in funding courses for these new practitioners reflected their interest in containing the rising costs of health care.

By 1974, there were 87 certificate programmes to prepare nurse practitioners (Watson Hawkins & Thibodeau, 1983). Reedy (1978) found that 38% of the existing nurse practitioner courses were preparation for child health care. By 1980, 58% of all programmes were awarding a master's degree to nurse practitioners, and Mauksh (1981) estimated that in 1981 there were about 14 000 nurse practitioners throughout the USA qualified to provide primary care.

The title 'nurse practitioner' was apparently not popular during the 1970s, 'nurse clinician' or 'clinical nurse specialist' often being preferred (Sultz et al, 1983). The title 'nurse practitioner' has become more acceptable in the 1980s, although there also appears to be some support for calling these nurses 'primary care nurses'. The American Nurses Association suggested in 1986 that the title 'nurse practitioner' should be phased out and cease to be used from 1992 onwards (Pearson & Stallmeyer, 1987). Wolcott Choi (1981) has discussed the intra- and interprofessional dissension surrounding the use of the term 'practitioner', and has suggested that:

'Placing emphasis on "practitioner" with a concomitant de-emphasis on "nurse" probably reveals underlying conflict about one's primary professional identity, value systems and allegiance.'   (Wolcott Choi, 1981)

The scope of practice of nurse practitioners

The first official definition of the nurse practitioner role came from the American Nurse's Association (ANA) in 1974. This definition was linked to statements concerning the educational needs of nurses with an expanded scope of practice (Allen, 1977; Watson Hawkins & Thibodeau, 1983). The 1975 guidelines for the Nurse Training Act, prepared in consultation with the ANA, define a nurse practitioner as 'a registered nurse who has successfully completed a formal program of study designed to prepare registered nurses to deliver primary health care including the ability to:

1   Assess the health status of individuals and families through health and medical history taking, physical examination and defining of health and developmental problems;
2   Institute and provide continuity of health care to clients (patients), work with the client to insure understanding of and compliance with the therapeutic regimen within established protocols, and recognise when to refer the client to a physician or other health care provider;
3   Provide instruction and counselling to individuals, families and groups in the areas of health promotion and maintenance, including involving such persons in planning for their health care; and
4   Work in collaboration with other health care providers and agencies to provide, and where appropriate, coordinate services to individuals and families.   (Bliss and Cohen, 1977)

In 1981, the ANA released their first Social Policy Statement, in which they defined the scope of nursing practice as 'the diagnosis and treatment of *human responses* to actual or potential health problems' (Watson Hawkins & Thibodeau, 1983). Fierce opposition to this statement from nurses in primary health care forced its removal in a second printing (Diers & Molde, 1983).

There were inevitable legal implications in defining the nurse practitioner role to include the performance of essentially medical tasks, such as diagnosis, treatment and prescription. Nurses in the USA are licensed and registered by the states in which they practice, and must satisfy the minimum requirements of training of those states. Each state usually includes a definition of nursing in its nurse practice act. These definitions are still in the process of being modified to allow for nurse practitioners' extended roles. The consequence of individual state legislature is a tremendous variation in nurses' roles. The following components of a nurse practitioner's work have been documented, and these vary from state to state:

● Obtain a complete health history
● Perform a complete physical examination

- Order laboratory tests and radiographs
- Make an initial diagnosis
- Perform minor surgery
- Use local infiltrating anaesthetics as necessary
- Write prescriptions on blanks pre-signed by doctors
- Telephone prescriptions to pharmacy
- Initiate and modify drug therapies using protocols
- Independently recommend non-prescription drugs
- Prescribe medication
- Dispense from samples and clinic stock

(Leitch & Sullivan Mitchell, 1977)

Screening, physical and psychosocial assessment and health promotion should be added to this list (Watson Hawkins & Thibodeau, 1983). Although roles may vary, patients of both physicians and nurse practitioners present equally complex medical problems. Where differences exist they lie in the type of person seen: nurse practitioners more often treat the chronically sick, the old, the poor, less 'desirable' patients such as alcoholics, and the mentally ill (Diers & Molde, 1983).

Junior doctoring or excellence in nursing?

The role of the physician's assistant was developing at the same time as that of the nurse practitioner. Many in the wider nursing profession felt that nurses who were extending their role to incorporate medical tasks were deserting the caring ethic of nursing in favour of a medical model (Skeet, 1978; Reeder & Mauksh, 1979).

Many failed to see a distinction between the role of nurse practitioner and physician's assistant and fears were expressed of nursing being 'consumed' by medicine (Barhydt-Wezenaar, 1981; Bates, 1970). However, several studies showed that doctors prefered to work with physician's assistants, who they perceived as posing less of a professional threat to them than nurse practitioners, since nursing is a professional domain independent of medicine (Johnson & Freeborn, 1986).

The perceived threat of nurse practitioners to mainsteam nursing in the early 1970s was fuelled by more than a third of nurse practitioner programmes being directed by non-nurses (usually doctors). By 1980, however, only 7% of programmes had non-nurses as heads (Sultz et al, 1983). Nursing slowly began to claim the extended role of the nurse practitioner as a legitimate part of nursing. In doing so nurses have had to consider what nursing is and what knowledge is necessary for its practice.

Ellis (1982) has suggested that the foci of care for medicine and nursing are different, medicine being primarily concerned with the diagnosis, treatment and cure of illness, while nursing's major concern is for the person and family as affected by the illness; nursing has a health rather than a disease focus. Allen and colleagues (1982) found that patients cared for by nurses who spent a significantly greater proportion of their time discussing their health rather than their illness felt that they had been helped over a life-changing event by nursing care.

There is considerable evidence that nurse practitioners offer care that is safe, effective and acceptable to patients (Wolcott Choi, 1981; Molde & Diers, 1985; see also Chapter 2).

Oucomes of nurse practitioner care

There is substantial evidence that nurse practitioners provide care equivalent to, and sometimes more effectively than, physicians (Sullivan, 1982). Sox (1979) reported that in 21 studies comparing primary health care by nurse practitioners with care by physicians, there were no differences between the two types of provider.

The care of patients with chronic diseases has shown particularly dramatic outcomes. Hypertensive patients attending nurse-run clinics achieved a significant reduction of blood pressure (Runyan, 1985; Ramsay et al, 1982). Watkins & Wagner (1982) found that nurses were more effective at getting people to lose weight, keep appointments and adhere to other recommendations. In a study of chronically ill elderly people in an inner-city area of Boston, it was found that those cared for by nurse practitioners were less likely to be admitted to hospital and more likely to be discharged early if they were admitted (Fagin, 1982).

Nurse practitioners can currently prescribe in 20 states. La Plante & O'Bannon (1987) found that the most frequently prescribed drugs were antibiotics, followed by anti-inflammatory drugs, antihistamines and decongestants. Upper respiratory tract infection was the most frequently reported health problem. The authors found that only 2% of their prescriptions were changed by nurse practitioners after consultation with a physician; they concluded that nurse practitioners have appropriate and safe prescribing practices.

Relationship with physicians

Although the development of the nurse practitioner role was a collaborative effort between medicine and nursing, this collaboration is less in evidence in the practice of health care: the directive approach is more characteristic of physician behaviour (Bates, 1970). Perhaps it is easier for doctor and nurse academics to negotiate a partnership style than it is for nurses in practice who are often employed by physicians (Buehler,1982).

Booth (a nurse) and Spicer (a doctor) (Booth, 1981) describe a practice that they founded at the University of Maryland which involved some clinical work, education and administration. Both speak highly of its success, despite conflict from time to time, and Booth attributes this success to direct open problem-solving, high standards and assertiveness. Assertiveness, however, is a new characteristic in nursing, and is only slowly developing with its newly found expression of self-worth (Mauksh, 1981). It is more difficult for nurses and doctors to collaborate as equals because they are divided by social class, sex and personality differences. Furthermore, hierarchical frameworks, particularly in hospitals, militate against real teamwork (Speedling, 1984). Although several studies report favourable attitudes of physicians towards nurse practitioners where they have worked with them, reluctance to give up authority and see the nurse as an independent professional has also been evident (Bullough, 1975; Watson Hawkins & Thibodeau, 1983). On the other hand, effective communication between the two professionals was thought by Spitzer *et al* (1974), in their randomised controlled trial of nurse practitioner care, to lead to more efficient working.

Although physician acceptance of nurse practitioners increased during the 1970s, it is now low: there is no longer a shortage of physicians and nurse practitioners are seen as a threat to their employment prospects (Freund, 1986). Clearly, relationships between doctors and nurses are complex and difficult to negotiate as roles change.

Patients' attitudes towards nurse practitioners

This is discussed more fully by Stilwell in Chapter 10. In short, research reveals that most patients who experience nurse practitioner care are satisfied and desire to continue with it. Patients prefer nurse practitioners to work with physicians.

Economic issues

Spitzer (1984) has suggested that nurse practitioners, by asking for larger salaries, are contributing to the death of their own role. The question of the economic impact of the nurse practitioner role is an important one for them. Freund (1986) suggests that there are three useful measures of nurse practitioners' economic impact: productivity, profitability and cost of care, although all three are interrelated.

Productivity is a measure of the nurse practitioner's effect on the output of a practice. Most studies have found an increase in productivity measured by the number of patient visits (see O'Hara-Devereaux *et al*, 1977; Seigal *et al*, 1977 for reviews).

The next step in economic evaluation is to look at profitability: does the nurse practitioner's increased productivity generate income? This is difficult to estimate because of the many possible ways of calculating costs. However, Freund (1986) reports that in all but one of the studies that she reviewed the practice income was increased.

Both profitability and cost of care issues are linked to direct reimbursement for nurse practitioner services. At present, American nurse practitioners generally cannot be paid directly for their services; they can only be paid via an employing physician. Legislation has been passed in several states now allowing third party payment to nurse practitioners, but the practice is far from common. It is the campaign for direct payment that has encouraged nurses to think politically.

The cost of care has been studied by comparing the costs of physician and nurse practitioner care: in all studies, cost of care by nurse practitioners has been found to be lower. Studies have found nurse practitioner care costs to be between 20% and 50% lower than the equivalent service given by a physician (Barhydt-Wezenaar, 1981).

On the other hand, as nurse practitioners are not always competing for the same market – nurse practitioners being more likely to see the chronically sick, the old, the poor – such costings provide too simplistic an economic analysis. Moreover, as nurse practitioners are placing more emphasis on preventive health care, and health promotion, it could be argued that this has a greater impact on cost saving than technological medicine (Fagin, 1982; Mezey, 1986).

The worldwide development of expanded roles for nurses

The expansion of the nurse's role in the USA stimulated other countries to consider similar developments, and a number of reports have drawn attention to the potential of nursing manpower in less developed countries (Rajan & Pang, 1978; Morrow & Amoako, 1980; Barhydt-Wezenaar, 1981; Seivwright, 1982; Ngcongo & Stark, 1986).

A further impetus to extend nursing roles was the 1978 Alma Ata declaration of 'Health for All by the Year 2000'. Jaeger-Burns (1981) expresses the commitment this represents from many countries in terms of improving their life expectancy which in sub-Saharan Africa is 43 years, in Asia 53 years and in Latin America 59 years. Life expectancy in Northern Europe and the USA is 72 years. Following the Alma Ata declaration, a meeting of nurses took place in 1981 in Geneva to consider the role of the nurse in achieving the goal of health for all. One of the recommendations made at the meeting was that concepts of primary health care should be included in nurse training curricula. It was also suggested that nurses should become active in policy-making for health, influencing governments and other health-related groups to act to set priorities (World Health Organization, 1982).

Botswana has encouraged independent nursing practice since 1965, when it became a republic. There were no doctors in the country at that time, except for a few medical missionaries. Ngcongo and Stark (1986) describe how nurses in Botswana took primary health care to rural populations because they were 'the most skilled cadre of health worker'. Over half the population live in villages of fewer than 500 inhabitants, usually with no road access. A family nurse practitioner programme has now been developed there with the intention of improving the quality and quantity of care: about 90% of the population now lives within 15 km of a health centre. With assistance from American nurse educators, a one-year family nurse practitioner training programme has been established. Family nurse practitioners are taught to manage health problems within the framework of the country's health services. There are 110 doctors in Botswana, and 1105 qualified nurse practitioners. There is apparently widespread acceptance of the nurse practitioner role partly because it has arisen from a logical expansion of the vital existing nursing services in Botswana.

A paediatric nurse practitioner course has also been set up in Ghana, to train nurses to provide primary health care services for children.

Morrow and Amoako (1980) say that 90 000 children die annually (out of 120 000) from diseases that could be prevented by immunisation, malaria prophylaxis or recognition of nutritional deficiency. The results of the course have not yet been evaluated, but the authors note that by the end of the course most nurses were handling cases competently and referring fewer patients to the physicians.

Rajan and Pang (1978) reported that nurse practitioners had also been introduced in Singapore, into clinics for sexually transmitted diseases. The aim was to assist doctors by relieving them of routine tasks. Apparently the clinical skills of the nurse practitioners in diagnosing sexually transmitted diseases matched those of the doctors. Patient waiting time was also reduced by 25%.

Seivwright (1982) described the introduction of nurse practitioners into the Jamaican health care system, based on the 'collective belief of Jamaican nurses that:

1   Access to adequate health care is a basic human right, not a privilege;
2   This care should be available to the individual at the time of need, regardless of his ability to pay; nursing forms an integral and indispensable part of health care services everywhere and must be available to individuals irrespective of nationality, race, colour, social status, creed or political affiliation;
3   The health care delivery system must reflect the inherent value of human life and the dignity of the individual;
4   The high values of every man, woman and child is a desirable goal;
5   The social and economic progress of any country bears a direct relationship to the health of the population.'

Largely for these reasons the nurse practitioner movement has been developed worldwide. The World Health Organization has pointed to the link between the objectives of nursing theory and those of the movement of health for all through primary health care (World Health Organization, 1986). The increasingly important role of nurses in preventive procedures and health promotion has already been discussed and it is easy to see the enormous potential that exists for nurses to improve health services in countries where provision is inadequate. The World Health Organization (1986) concluded that nursing theories can guide nursing practice and help to achieve the targets for Health for All and ends by saying:

> 'The extent of the role of nursing in the achievement of the targets and in the direction of its own future depends, in part, on organisational strength, the quality of the health service design and the political will of the people. What will nurses choose to do?'

References

Allen A (1977) Credentialing of continuing education nurse practitioner programmes. In Bliss A A & Cohen E D (eds) *The New Health Professionals*. Maryland: Aspen Systems Corporation

Allen M, Frassure Smith N & Gottlieb L (1982) What makes a 'good' nurse? *Canadian Nurse*, **78**, 42–45

Barhydt-Wezenaar N (1981) *Nursing in Health Care Delivery in the United States*. New York: Jonas S Springer

Bates B (1970) Doctor and nurse: changing roles and relations. *New England Journal of*

Medicine, **283**, 129–134

Bliss A A & Cohen E D (1977) (eds) *The New Health Professionals*. Maryland: Aspen Systems Corporation

Booth R Z (1981) Joint practice: concept and implementation, Part I. In Mauksch I G (ed) *Primary Care: A Contemporary Nursing Perspective*. New York: Grune and Stratton

Buehler J (1982) *Nurses and Physicians in Transition*. Michigan: UMI Research Press

Bullough B (1975) Barrier to the nurse practitioner movement: problems of women in a woman's field. *International Journal of Health Services*, **5**, 225–233

Curwen M H (1964) Lord Moran's ladder. *Journal of the Royal College of General Practitioners*, **7**, 38–65

Diers D & Molde S (1983) Nurses in primary care: the new gatekeepers. *American Journal of Nursing*, **83**, 742–745

Ellis R (1982) Conceptual issues in nursing. *Nursing Outlook*, **30**, 406–410

Fagin C M (1982) Nursing as an alternative to high cost care. *American Journal of Nursing*, **82**, 56–60

Fisher D W & Horowitz S M (1977) The physician's assistant: profile of a new health professional. In Bliss A A & Cohen E D (eds) *The New Health Professionals*. Maryland: Aspen Systems Corporation

Freund C M (1986) Nurse practitioners in primary care. In Mezey M D & McGivern D G (eds) *Nurses, nurse practitioners. The Evolution of Primary Care*. Boston: Little Brown

Jaeger-Burns J (1981) The relationship of nursing to primary health care internationally. *International Nursing Review*, **28**, 167–175

Johnson R E & Freeborn D K (1986) Comparing HMO physicians' attitudes towards NPs and PAs. *Nurse Practitioner*, **11**, 39–49

La Plante L J & O'Bannon F V (1987) NP prescribing recommendations. *Nurse Practitioner*, **2**, 19–30

Leitch C & Sullivan Mitchell M A (1977) State by state report: the legal accommodation of nurses practising in expanded roles. *Nurse Practitioner*, **2**, 19–30

Mauksh I G (1981) Nurse–physician collaboration: a changing relationship. *Journal of Nursing Administration*, **11**, 35–38

Mezey M D (1986) The future of primary care and nurse practitioners. In Mezey M D & McGivern D D (eds) *Nurses, Nurse practitioners. The Evolution of Primary Care*. Boston: Little Brown

Molde S & Diers D (1985) Nurse practitioner research: selected literature review and research agenda. *Nursing Research*, **34**, 362–367

Morrow H & Amoako D (1980) An expanded role for nurses as paediatric health care providers in Ghana. *International Nursing Review*, **27**, 76–78

Ngcongo V N & Stark R D (1986) The development of a family nurse practitioner programme in Botswana. *International Nursing Review*, **33**, 9–14

O'Hara Devereaux M, Dervin J V , Hughes L *et al* (1977) Economic effectiveness of family nurse practitioner practice in primary care in California. In Bliss A A & Cohen E D (eds) *The New Health Professionals*. Maryland: Aspen Systems Corporation

Pearson L (1985) Perspectives 20 years later from the pioneers of the NP movement. *Nurse Practitioner*, **10**, 15–18

Pearson L & Stallmeyer J (1987) Opposition to title change overwhelming. *Nurse Practitioner*, **12**, 10–15

Raffel M W (1980) *The US Health System Origins and Functions*. New York: Wiley

Rajan V S & Pang R (1978) Nurse practitioner in sexually transmitted diseases. *Nursing Journal of Singapore*, **18**, 73–76

Ramsay J, McKenzie J & Fish D (1982) Physicians and nurse practitioners: do they provide equal health care? *American Journal of Public Health*, **72**, 55–57

Reeder S & Mauksh H (1979) Nursing: continuing change. In Freeman H E, Levine S & Reeder L G. *Handbook of Medical Sociology*. New York: Prentice Hall

Reedy B L (1978) *The New Health Practitioners in America – a Comparative Study*. London: King Edward's Hospital Fund for London

Rogers D E (1977) The challenge of primary care. In Knowles J H (ed) *Doing Better and Feeling Worse. New York: W M Norton*

Runyan J W (1975) The Memphis Chronic Disease Program: comparisons in outcome and the nurse's extended role. Journal of the American Medical Association, **231**, 264–267

Seigal B, Jensen D A & Coffee E M (1977) Cost effectiveness of FNP versus MD staffed rural practice. In Bliss A A & Cohen E D (eds) *The New Health Professionals* Maryland: Aspen Systems Corporation

Seivwright M J (1982) Nurse practitioners in Primary care in Jamaica. *International Nursing Review*, **29**, 22–24

Silver H K, Ford L C & Stearly S G (1967) A program to increase health care for children – the paediatric nurse practitioner program. *Paediatrics*, **39**, 756–760

Skeet M (1978) Health auxiliaries: decision makers and implementers. In Skeet M & Elliott K (eds) *Health Auxiliaries and the Health Team*. London: Croom Helm

Sox H C (1979) Quality of patient care by nurse practitioners and physicians: a ten year perspective. *Annals of Internal medicine*, **91**, 459–468

Speedling E J (1984) Nurse–physician collaboration: a review of some carriers to its fulfillment. *Bulletin of the New York Academy of Medicine*, **60**, 811–818

Spitzer W O (1984) The nurse practitioner re-visited: slow death of a good idea. *New England Journal of Medicine*, **310**, 104–105

Spitzer W O, Sackett D L, Sibley J C *et al* (1974) The Burlington randomised trial of the nurse practitioner. *New England Journal of Medicine*, **290**, 251-256

Sullivan J (1982) Research on nurse practitioners: process behind the outcome? *American Journal of Public Health*, **72**, 8–9

Sultz H A, Henry O M, Kinyon L J *et al* (1983) Nurse practitioner: a decade of change. *Nursing outlook*, **31**, 216–219

Watkins L & Wagner E (1982) Nurse practitioner and physician adherence to standing orders: criteria for consultation or referral. *American Journal of Public Health*, **72**, 55–57

Watson Hawkins J B & Thibodeau J A (1983) *The Nurse Practitioner: Current Practice Issues*, New York: Tiresias Press

Wolcott Choi M (1981) Nurses as co-providers of primary health care. *Nursing Outlook*, **29**, 519–521

World Health Organization (1982) *Report of a Meeting on Nursing in Support of the Goal of Health for All by the Year 2000, 16–18 November 1981*. Geneva: WHO

World Health Organization (1986) *Nursing discussion paper*, Copenhagen: WHO

2

The Changing Role of the Practice Nurse in the UK – from Doctor's Assistant to Collaborative Practitioner

ANN BOWLING

Practice nurses: definition, organisation and numbers

Practice nurses are generally state registered nurses, who are employed by general practitioners (GPs) to perform clinical and preventive health care procedures in the surgery. There is some overlap with the role of the district nurse. District nurses give nursing care mainly in the patient's home, but may treat their mobile patients in the GP's surgery. Some combine their surgery work with a more clinical role where GPs do not employ their own practice nurses. In these circumstances they perform treatments for patients referred to them by the GPs while they are carrying out their surgery sessions. However, they rarely spend more than a few hours a week in the practices (Reedy *et al*, 1980).

Most health authorities attach district nurses to general practices, where they are responsible for providing home (community) nursing care for the patients registered with the GPs. In some urban areas, where GPs' patients span a wide catchment area, the district nurses are geographically organised, an arrangement that is more economical in terms of their travelling time, but they have less direct contact with the GPs and involvement in the surgery. In the case of health centres, health authorities may attach a treatment room nurse to provide agreed surgery treatments requested by the GPs. Most GPs in health centres, however, rely on district nurses manning the treatment room on a rota basis.

Since the mid-1960s, family practitioner committees (FPC) have been able to reimburse GPs with 70% of the salary costs of up to two non-medical staff, including nurses, per principal.

There has been a substantial increase in the numbers of practice nurses over the past decade, although the overall number is still small (Fig. 2.1). This increase is probably partly due to the large amount of publicity GPs' journals (such as *Pulse*) now give to the role of the nurse. It is frequently pointed out that nurses can pay for their 30% salary cost, and even benefit the practice financially, by performing item for service tasks (e.g. immunisations/vaccinations, cervical smears) for which the GP is paid by the family practitioner committee (Bowling 1987a).

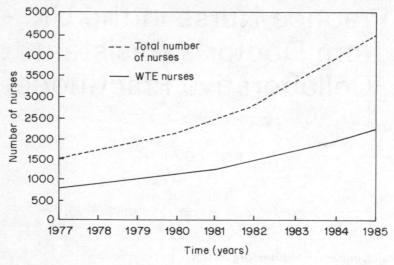

Fig. 2.1 Numbers of practice nurses, 1977-85

A small body of professionals, called facilitators, has also emerged in recent years with the aim of encouraging GPs to work with nurses to provide preventive health care (Bowling, 1987b). A number of general practitioners have begun to employ nurses to manage systematic screening clinics and follow-up care for cardiovascular preventive programmes.

In 1985 there were 2211 full-time equivalent practice nurses, consisting of 4392 nurses working, on average, 18 hours a week. In contrast there were about 26 000 GPs (a ratio of 12 GPs to one practice nurse). The shortfall in the number of practice nurses is further demonstrated when analysing the number of practice nurses per head of population in each Regional Health Authority (Table 2.1). Table 2.1 shows that Mersey, for example, had 48 whole time equivalent practice nurses (1 per 50 585 population) while East Anglia had 202 (1 per 9601 population) (Bowling, 1987). The number of district nurses per head of population, in most regions, in contrast, is between 1 : 2 000 and 1 : 3 000 (the ideal is 1 : 2 000).

Table 2.1   Numbers of GP-employed practice nurses (WTE) by region in England, 1985
(Source: DHSS, Statistics and Research Division)

RHA	No. of GP-employed nurses(whole time equivalent)	No. in population per practice nurse
Mersey	48	50 585
North Western	74	54 009
Yorks	117	30 759
Northern	130	23 793
South East Thames	133	27 032
South West Thames	135	21 880
Oxford	153	15 721
North East Thames	180	20 768
Trent	182	25 332
Wessex	183	15 433
East Anglia	202	9 601
South Western	203	15 394
West Midlands	275	18 821
Total	2211	

What do practice nurses do?

Surveys of the work of practice nurses and treatment room nurses have shown that they perform a wide range of technical procedures (Bowling, 1981; Reedy, 1972; Reedy *et al*, 1980). Table 2.2 lists 45 tasks that Reedy (1972) found reported in the literature as being performed by practice nurses. Cater and Hawthorn (Chapter 9) found that practice nurses in the Nottinghamshire area performed a range of the more technical procedures and were also beginning to adopt a preventive screening role (e.g. cardiovascular risk factor identification), in contrast to district nurses and nurses attached to work in health centre treatment rooms and employed by the district health authority. Greenfield *et al* (1987) also found practice nurses in the West Midlands performing a wide range of technical tasks, from blood pressure measurement to cervical smears. They found also that over half reported currently making observations of the skin to detect signs of disease, over half reported examining breasts, over half managed uncomplicated minor injuries and hypertension and almost half managed simple allergies.

There is a wide variation in the attitudes of nurses and GPs towards extended nurses' roles and suitable tasks for transfer (Bowling, 1981, 1985a, 1985b). Table 2.3 shows those tasks most often approved of by nurse management in district health authorities (DHA) for inclusion within the extended role of the nurse (re: district nurses and treatment room nurses). The variation is wide.

Although most practice nurses undertake mainly clinical 'treatment' tasks, a number of practices have been developing this role into that of 'prevention nurse'. Such practice nurses may run clinics (e.g. well woman), monitor blood pressure, give health education and advice and carry out health checks. This role requires a high level of responsibility (in terms of making initial assessments, appropriate referrals and planning care) and administrative and clinical skill. This role is being monitored by Fullard *et al* (1984). Some practice nurses also see self-referred patients (without the patient first consulting the GP), although they are currently untrained for this extended role, which inevitably involves them in making initial diagnostic assessments.

Table 2.2   Delegated tasks (Reedy, 1972)

In his article, The General Practice Nurse, Barry Reedy listed 45 tasks which he found had been delegated by doctors to nurses at one time or another in a number of surgeries:

Height and weight measurement
Temperature, pulse and respiration rate
Blood pressure recording
Chemical testing of urine and faeces
Supervising the collection of urine and
    faeces for the laboratory
Bacteriological sampling for transmission
    to the laboratory
Estimation of ESR and haemoglobin
    within the practice
Venepuncture
Immunology performance of Planotest
Performance of cervical smears
Electrocardiography
Audiometry
Tonometry
Use of peak flow meter and vitalograph
Ear-syringing and other aural treatments
    and dressings
Application of plasters and cervical
    collars
Application of splints
Changing vaginal pessaries
Simple physiotherapy
Counselling
Supervision of certain types of patient
Dietary supervision
Advising receptionists over patients'
    needs
Chaperoning

Preparation of patients for doctor and
    assisting at examination of treatment
Liaison with hospital in-patients and
    laboratory
Maintenance and care of equipment,
    dressing, drugs and linen
Supervision of sterilisation and antisepsis
    procedures
Transport of patients to and from surgery
Reception and assessment of patients
    attending without appointments
Initial home visits
Revisits
Routine visiting of chronic sick
Surgical dressings
Insertion of sutures
Removal of sutures
Incision of boils and abscesses
Aspiration of cysts
Therapeutic injections (subcutaneous and
    intramuscular)
Immunisations and vaccinations
    (including smallpox)
Skin testing for allergy
Desensitising injections
Teaching patients illness management
    and hygiene
Supervision of certain clinics
Dispensing in rural practices

A small proportion of practice nurses feel that they are already operating within a nurse practitioner role of the type developed in the USA (Chapter 9). Greenfield *et al* (1987) found 80% of practice nurses in the West Midlands to be satisfied with their present role, although many felt that they were already acting within an extended nursing role. Fifteen per cent of the nurses in their sample wished to extend their role further. This has been a controversial issue over the last decade, with some members of the nursing profession fearing that such developments may make nurses more subservient to doctors.

Table 2.3 Tasks most commonly approved by nurse managers as being within the 'extended' role of nurses employed by the DHA (*n* = 122 DHAs)

	No. of DNSs (Community) officially approving performance of task	%
Immunisation/vaccination (includes tuberculin Heaf testing)	112	92
Taking blood (venepuncture)	100	82
Ear syringing	71	58
Suturing certain skin lacerations	30	25
Family planning procedures: insertion/check IUCD, giving repeat prescriptions – FP advice only (1), pregnancy testing only (1)	13	11
Allergy testing/desensitising injections	23	47
Administration of drugs, (usually intravenous, also controlled and cytotoxic)	57	47
Cervical smears	16	13

There is variation between DHAs in the types of tasks nurse managers accept within the extended nurse role (for their district and treatment room nurses), and therefore in the degree of restriction imposed on their activities. The implication is that many privately employed practice nurses are experimenting more freely with their roles, while those employed by DHAs are often not permitted to do so (Bowling, 1985b; Royal College of General Practitioners, 1987).

The degree of variation in the nurse's role in the surgery between practices and districts is as great as the variation in the nurse practitioner's role between states in the USA, where the nurse practitioner's legal scope of practice is regulated by individual state legislature (Leitch & Sullivan Mitchell,1977).

The changing status of nursing: implications for extended roles

Traditionally, nurses have accepted instructions from their nursing superiors and from doctors, and have initiated only routine procedures. Their tradition of low status, relatively short and apprentice-based training, and female socialisation has reinforced this acceptance in the past (Wilson Barnett, 1986). As a result, leading representatives of the nursing profession have, until recently, been hostile toward extended nurse roles which have encompassed taking on more medical tasks (Bowling, 1981).

Thus the Royal College of Nursing a decade ago would only approve of 'delegation' (a term which itself implies transfer of work from a superior to a colleague of lesser status) if it was not detrimental to the interests of nursing (Royal College of Nursing, 1977, 1979). The mixed feelings, and intra- as well as inter-profession-al disagreements, among GPs and nurses about the content of the practice nurse's role in the late 1970s has been documented by Bowling (1981). This will not be repeated here, although it should be pointed out that it was clear from these anal-yses that feelings of professional (role) threat were evident in this opposition.

The demands for improved health care, the emphasis on caring in chronic ill-ness, and the trends towards preventive health care approaches have led to incentives to change and expand the role of the nurse in primary care. The World Health Organization's objective of 'Health for All by the Year 2000' will necessi-tate nurses in primary care becoming involved in the promotion and facilitation of healthy lifestyles, reducing the burden of preventable ill-health by implement-ing screening programmes and giving health education (World Health Organization, 1985). The gradual realisation of the potential power involved in an expanded nurse role has led to recent attitude changes among the nursing profession in the UK. The recent DHSS review team's report of community nursing services in England (Cumberlege Report: Department of Health and Social Security, 1986) supported the Royal College of Nursing's evidence in favour of the development of a nurse practitioner role (Royal College of Nursing, 1985) (see Chapter 3).

These attitude changes have mirrored those occurring among the nursing profession in the USA over the past decade. Representatives of the nursing profes-sion in the USA often voiced the opinion that nurse practitioners were 'defectors' from nursing, undermining nursing in the process (Watson Hawkins & Thibodeau, 1983; Diers & Molde, 1983). The nurse practitioner movement in the USA, and now in the UK, has forced nurse educators to think more critically about the philosophical underpinnings of the profession: What is nursing? What knowledge is required for its practice and for its acceptance as an independent profession alongside medicine? (see Stilwell, Chapter 1, for a full discussion of this issue).

Some nurses educators in the USA soon recognised the value of physical exam-ination skills and added these to nursing degree programmes. These skills, aided by the tools of the otoscope, ophthalmoscope and stethoscope, gave nurses increased knowledge, responsibility and accountability. Nurses who can per-form their own physical examinations are less reliant on the doctor and, in effect, can control the doctor's entree to the patient (Diers & Molde, 1983).

The Royal College of Nursing (RCN) in the UK has now realised the power involved in being a gatekeeper of primary care, alongside the doctor. The RCN justifies its recent endorsement of a nurse practitioner role in the UK by pointing to public need, although the attractions of the role, in terms of increasing profes-sional status and power, must also be apparent to them:

'The provision of a nurse practitioner service would lead to earlier identification and treatment of problems as well as encouraging prevention of illness and promo-tion of health.'   (Royal College of Nursing, 1987)

In order to provide this service the RCN called for increased autonomy – a need for:

'an autonomous nursing service reflecting a level of nursing competency which enables and requires the practitioner to be fully accountable for her work. This must include responsibility for accepting and discharging patients; for planning, implementing and evaluating the programme of care; and for referring patients to other practitioners as necessary.'   (Royal College of Nursing, 1987).

This again mirrors developments in the USA where the profession indicates more openly the benefits of autonomy for its members:

'Primary care is and always has been nursing... The struggle for control of that field is the issue for the '80s. For primary care is the gate through which people enter the health care system, and she who controlleth the gate controlleth it all.'(Diers, 1982)

Many nurse practitioners in the USA operate in similar areas of patient care as district nurses in the UK, but with far more autonomy and scope of practice. They are now setting up their own private nurse practitioner clinics. So in the USA there are nurse practitioners who do home visiting, who specialise in care of the elderly, children and various chronic conditions as well as providing acute and preventive health care.

If nurses simply take over the menial chores of doctors, it is then difficult to just-ify the nurse's role as 'nursing'. Thus, the focus of the nurse practitioner movement is not the medical diagnosis, but the response to 'whole patient care'. It is increas-ingly important for nurses to be able to demonstrate the differences in approach, given the economics of the threatened surplus of doctors (Spitzer, 1984).

Nurse practitioners in the USA and many practice nurses in the UK stress that the extended clinical role does not make them into half-fledged doctors – primary care provided by nurses is different from care given by doctors. The differences, however, are difficult to define. One difference is that the nurse's role is more comprehensive than that of a physician's assistant, and involves professional responsibility and judgement within her own field. The nurse practi-tioner is responsible for assessment and implementation of nursing care needs (Bates, 1970).

The debate over roles and professional autonomy partly results from the fact that both medicine and nursing have an overlapping knowledge base because they both study disease and its treatment. In one sense, nurse practitioners and practice nurses with extended roles *are* doctor substitutes, but they appear to be more than that.

There is a vast literature in the USA demonstrating patient satisfaction with and acceptance of nurse practitioner care, indicating that nurses can manage patients with chronic conditions and provide preventive health care as effectively as, and in some cases more effectively than, doctors. (For examples of studies and fuller reviews of the literature see Flyn, 1974; Spitzer *et al*, 1974; Pesznecker & Draye, 1978; Storms & Fox, 1979; Manisoff, 1979; Gerdes, 1980; Ramsay *et al*, 1980; Bowling, 1981; Cintron *et al*, 1983; Spitzer, 1984; Mezey & McGivern, 1986; Molde & Diers, 1985.)

Over the last decade, the number of published studies of nurse practitioner practice in the USA has declined: with their increasing acceptance there is less need to justify their presence. Molde and Diers (1985) have drawn attention to the need for more research into the process of nurse practitioner care to identify *why* nurses have higher success rates than doctors in helping patients lose weight, comply with advice, control their blood pressure and so on. Is nurse practitioner care different from care provided by doctors or do nurses simply spend more time with patients, which explains their success in these areas (Bessman, 1974; Flyn, 1974); see also Chapter 1 for a fuller discussion of this issue)?

Although the literature on the scope of the practice nurse's role in the UK is increasing, mirroring the state of research in the USA in the 1960s and 1970s, as yet little has been published in the UK on the quality or outcome of practice nurses' care.

The role of the nurse in both nations is changing in an attempt to be more responsive to societal needs and demands for improved health care. The most common patient presenting problem now seen by nurse practitioners in the USA is prevention and health supervision, followed by respiratory conditions. Nurse practitioner caseloads include older, more chronically sick patient populations. They manage more females, people in ethnic minority groups, and those on low incomes than do physicians (Molde & Diers, 1985). The implication appears to be that they are treating patients whom doctors find less attractive.

In response, Mezey and McGivern (1986) have referred to Florence Nightingale to support their argument that preventive care and treatment of all populations is within the legitimate domain of nursing:

> '...nursing proper is... to help the patient suffering from disease to live – just as health nursing is to keep or put the constitution of the healthy child or human being in such a state as to have no disease'   (Nightingale, 1893).

So nursing has asserted that it has always occupied this primary care and preventive role. It is identifying the role more clearly now in an attempt to meet changing health care needs of society, to contain the costs of health care delivery and present its members with roles more consistent with their background and training (Mezey & McGivern, 1986).

Ironically, although nurses are referring to Nightingale in an attempt to justify their extending roles, it was Nightingale who also set a precedent for the subordinate role of nurses within the medical hierarchy. She refused to allow the nurses under her command to give any care to wounded soldiers until the surgeons ordered them to do so (Woodham-Smith, 1951).

By many accounts, however, nurse practitioner programmes were developed to alleviate doctor shortages and maldistributions (Mezey & McGivern, 1986); (see also Chapter 1). Similarly, in the UK the early literature on the work of practice nurses concentrated on how the practice nurse could save the doctor's time (Royal College of General Practitioners, 1968; Hodgkin, 1967; Hasler *et al*, 1968; Kuenssberg, 1971).

Developments in training: USA and UK comparisons

The first formal education programme for nurse practitioners in the USA started in 1965 at the University of Colorado, in the face of opposition from many nursing and medical professionals (Storms, 1973). At the same time Duke University began a certificate programme for physician's assistants. By the late 1960s the literature frequently expressed the need to stimulate the development of new categories of health workers. Although at first US nursing schools were reluctant to develop such programmes and to include diagnosis in their curricula, attitudes gradually changed (see Chapter 1 for an overview of the development of the USA nurse practitioner role). Federal Acts of 1964, 1968 and 1975 provided finance for advance nurse training and the establishment of nurse practitioner programmes. By 1976 an American Nurses Association programme was implemented to provide for certification of nurses as nurse practitioners. Thus in little over a decade the concept of extended nurse roles had led to a new definition of practice, and about 2 000 nurse practitioners now graduate per annum (Golden, 1979). Nurses have sought changes in state legislation where practice is restricted. Many states have revised their laws and are acting as a stimulus and example to other states – a momentum for change has developed (Bullough, 1976).

In the UK there are no legal constraints on the nurse's role, with the exception of prescribing. Also, unlike the USA, no finance has so far been forthcoming from professional bodies (e.g. the Royal College of Nursing) or the DHSS to fund courses for practice nurses in either traditional or extended roles. Most district health authorities offer study days or individual tuition for the nurses in their employment, as required, on procedures such as immunisations/vaccinations, ear syringing and venepuncture. The training is given either by senior nurses or by doctors. Nurses undergoing this tuition will, having successfully completed it, be issued with a certificate of competence to undertake the specified task. Some DHAs will extend this tuition to practice nurses employed by GPs (Bowling, 1985b). Apart from short courses organised locally by groups of practice nurses, by local faculties of the Royal College of General Practitioners, and more recently by some colleges of further education and polytechnics, little training has been available.

Previously the Joint Board for Clinical Nursing Studies has repeatedly refused to recommend a national course with a uniform curriculum.

It is held that courses should be designed locally to meet local needs. In practice this has led to role confusion, with nurses in different practices and districts undertaking different procedures, and to a paucity of adequate training courses.

The Royal College of Nursing, in its response to the DHSS's reports on Primary Health Care and the Community Nursing Review (Cumberlege Report), recommended that DHAs should provide practice nurse training as an interim measure until mandatory training, which it recommends, has been introduced (Royal College of Nursing, 1987). The Royal College of General Practitioners, in its document responding to the Cumberlege Report, expressed the hope that members (general practitioners) of local faculties of the RCGP would contribute to this education (Royal College of General Practitioners, 1987).

Nurse training generally is currently being reconsidered, and ultimately this may have implications for the training of practice nurses. The professional body regulating nursing is known as the United Kingdom Central Council for Nursing,

Midwifery and Health Visiting (UKCC). In the report *Project 2000: A New Preparation for Practice* (1986), the UKCC proposed a new three year common nurse training resulting in a new nurse who would undertake much of the work of the present two levels of nurse (enrolled and registered). In addition, nurses wishing to become 'specialist practitioners' would undergo further preparation. It is possible that the specialist courses will be expanded to include recognised courses for practice nurses.

The Royal College of Nursing, in its document on training needs of practice nurses, provided guidelines for an outline curriculum for practice nurses (Royal College of Nursing, 1984). This is evidence of the RCN's changing (more positive) attitude towards extended nursing roles. The proposals included education on interpersonal communication, preventive health care, clinical skills, psychology and clinical decision making. The procedures recommended for inclusion were:

- Collection, handling and transportation of laboratory specimens
- Venepuncture
- Electrocardiography
- Immunisation (adults and children); other injections and vaccines; desensitising procedures
- Screening procedures such as blood pressure, cervical cytology, breast examination, skin testing, vitalography, peak flow meter
- Preparation of eye for examination; common eye treatments and removal of foreign bodies
- Examination and common treatments of the ear; use of the auriscope; ear syringing
- Application of special dressings and bandages, surgical collars and other orthopaedic appliances
- Family planning: basic knowledge of contraceptive methods; basic information about sterilisation, termination of pregnancy and infertility
- First aid and management of emergencies, such as: cardiac arrest; injuries – sprains, fractures, wounds; haemorrhage; anaphylactic shock; inhalation of foreign bodies; ingestions of poisonous substances; burns and scalds; fainting
- Drugs: controlled drugs – use and misuse; pharmacology of common drugs; drug reactions and interactions
- Recognition and treatment of simple skin conditions
- Knowledge and nursing care of: minor ailments and simple medical conditions; upper respiratory tract infections; urinary tract infections; gastroenteritis

The RCN's interest in, and commitment to, extended nurse roles, which include diagnostic and assessment as well as nursing care and clinical skills, is evident from this list.

The UKCC (via the English National Board (ENB) subsection) has recently drawn up guidelines for practice nurse courses. These include the requirement that they should be held in institutions currently approved to offer district nursing and health visiting courses, and that the courses are evaluated. Currently, approximately 15 courses in such institutions (in colleges of further education and polytechnics) have been approved by the ENB. These courses are generally organised on a day release basis but are very short (spanning about 10–15 days) and nurses completing them are awarded a certificate of attendance. The courses approved by the ENB follow the guidelines of the RCN but rarely include the more advanced diagnostic and treatment skills. This omission reflects the short length of the courses and inadequate funding, as well as the different opinions among nurses about what skills are appropriate for inclusion in extended roles. Thus, personal bias is still influential in role development.

The problem of funding remains. Practice nurses either pay their own fees or they are paid by the GPs they work for: there is no source of grant funding. In theory, under Section 63 of the GP's reimbursement scheme, practice nurses can reclaim from the family practitioner committee two-thirds of their expenses where courses are held on health authority or related premises. In practice, FPCs across England interpret the rules differently, with some reimbursing part of the course fees and some only partly reimbursing subsistence costs.

In conclusion, the Royal College of Nursing has at least decided which procedures are within the legitimate role of practice nurses, but it is doubtful whether its recommendations will be fully implemented until a national training course with a uniform curriculum is available. For the full professional recognition of practice nursing as a legitimate area of practice this accreditation is essential. This would not only provide the public with safe and effective care – the hallmark of professional accountability – but will protect and therefore benefit the members of the profession. It will also enable the nurse to be accountable for his/her own actions and therefore increase autonomy.

Accountability and autonomy

An essential behaviour that practice nurses need to acquire for their newly developing role is a sense of autonomy (a sense of self) and self accountability. It is this that distinguishes the nurse practitioner in the USA from other nurses (Mauksch, 1978).

The nurse's ability to relate to the doctor as an equal professional has been handicapped by the fact that most doctors are men and most nurses are women in a society traditionally socialised to believe that men were the decision makers. Health care settings are often a microcosm of society as a whole. There are attempts to change this, particularly among nurse educators but this is inevitably difficult.

The doctor must learn to understand the nurse's competencies, and to respect the nurse professionally. The nurse must learn to be accountable for his/her own judgement, and stop expecting the doctor to be accountable and responsible for his/her activities. Nurses must carry their own liability insurance and be willing to take calculated risks. For this to be achieved, the nurse must be clear about his/her competence and area of expertise (Mauksch, 1978).

In the UK the practice nurse is less likely to be legally protected, by virtue of RCN or trade union membership, than health authority employed nurses

(Bowling, 1985b). This is one undesirable consequence of their employment outside the mainstream of nursing. More disturbing is their lack of concern about their legal cover: many feel that the doctor's insurance covers them adequately, and that therefore the doctor takes responsibility for their actions (Bowling, 1985b). Although the Medical Defence Union's legal liability insurance scheme for doctors can include cover for the GP in the event of a mishap by a practice nurse this is not adequate in a case of negligence by a practice nurse. The legal status for practice nurses has never been clearly defined although the DHSS, the Medical Defence Union and the (then) Queen's Institute of District Nursing have all issued guidelines:

'The doctor is responsible for any negligence on the part of the nurse when the latter is acting in the doctor's presence, carrying out the doctor's treatment, and when under the doctor's direct supervision'

'When the doctor allows the nurse to perform delegated duties in his/her own way, then the nurse is liable for negligence.'   (Medical Defence Union, 1970; Queen's Institute of District Nursing, 1970)

'The doctor may be guilty of negligence if authority was conferred on a nurse to perform a task outside the scope of normal duties, or for which he/she had no special qualification.'

'The nurse may be held legally liable if he/she has failed to exercise skills properly expected, or if the nurse has undertaken tasks he/she is not competent to perform.' (Department of Health and Social Security, 1977)

Unfortunately this is the level of the debate in the UK – instead of attempting to make the nurse totally responsible for his/her own actions and therefore an autonomous practitioner. At least the RCN's list of tasks suitable for inclusion in practice nurse courses can be claimed to be nursing duties in the future – rather than 'delegated' medical tasks. This is one step in the right direction towards increased nurse autonomy and accountability. To achieve this, however, inter-professional respect and collaboration must be enhanced.

Facilitating interprofessional respect

Professional characteristics that form barriers to a collaborative practice can be difficult to change. It may be difficult for doctors not to be team leaders and hard for nurses to relinquish a subordinate role. The expanded role now offers an incentive to attempt change. There must be an understanding and recognition of each professional's skills and abilities. Territoriality is both a necessary ingredient and a potential barrier to collaboration. Each professional's perspective must be respected and professional identity preserved.

The minimum requirements for effective role expansion within practice nursing are summarised in Table 2.4. Many examples of these barriers, based on interviews with doctors and nurses, are given by Bowling (1981).

Table 2.4   Minimum requirements for effective task transfer between general practitioners and nurses

Inefficient task transfer	Efficient task transfer
GP barriers Lethargy Concern for prestige Fear of being superseded Lack of faith in others 'Over-interest' in the job	Identification of the problem(s), cause(s), solution(s) Joint control/agreement over practice Correct choice of tasks to be transferred Correct choice of staff type to perform task and staff compatibility Reallocation of responsibility together with task

Nurse barriers
Lack of: Risk taking
       Assertiveness
       Autonomy
	Discussion: consultative–participative style

Nurse management barriers Restriction on nurse activities due to: Reluctance to see GP paid twice for vaccinations, etc. (item-for-service tasks) Professionalisation: nurses should not perform medical tasks/do doctor's work/account to doctors	
Staff morale Minimum performance Demotivation Boredom/dissatisfaction Frustration Role misunderstandings	*Staff morale* Role understanding Training needs established/ongoing Ongoing potential for new skill development

If it can be assumed that extended nurse roles will lead to more extensive patient services, of equal or better quality than at present, then one main concern is how to change attitudes that are currently reinforcing the status quo. Recognition of the barriers to change by the professionals concerned will facilitate the ability to change among those willing to do so. In addition, nurses need to possess three characteristics that are incompatible with traditional nurse behaviour:

1   Risk taking – involved in an equal partnership with the doctor: the recording of observations of the patient and subsequent intervention;
2   Assertiveness – underlying the presentation of self as a professional of equal competence; the expression of his/her perspective of patient care priorities; expression of self-worth;
3   Autonomous intervention – accountability for one's own actions, rather than being covered by the doctor; the willingness to act independently without referral to the doctor.

(Mauksch, 1981)

Doctors' perceptions of nurses as subordinate rather than equal colleagues are unlikely to change until nurses change their behaviour. More attention also needs to be paid to the concept of 'teamwork' (collaborative patient care) in medical and nursing education before interprofessional collaboration can be effective (Bond *et al*, 1985).

The issue is not simply about enhancing the status of the nurse. It is about providing a more efficient health service for patients, in terms of the quantity of care available and its quality. Management experts have well known tactics for remedying inefficient methods of working (Goodworth, 1985). Management techniques would involve each professional in a primary care setting being prepared to do the following:

Identify the problem

A simple question can be asked: are there any procedures that would benefit patient care and all concerned if they were reallocated to self or others? The procedure should be transferred to the person most suited in terms of training, experience and proficiency. To transfer duties, roles and work priorities have to be defined. Duties and procedures have to be categorised into those falling clearly within an existing role and those safely falling outside it or within a 'grey' area. Professionals should jointly decide which can be shared or transferred.

Gather all the relevant facts

These include personal barriers such as lethargy, fear of being superseded, lack of confidence in others, a consuming interest in the job.

This part of the exercise then requires staff to think in turn about each staff member:

- What is that person's role?
- What are his/her strengths and weaknesses?
- In what areas has there been a failure to recognise and utilise that person's strengths?
- Establish the cause of the problem – the difficult task of self analysis (motivations, personal outlook and habit).
- Search for and develop possible solution.

In management, analysis of work content and reallocation of tasks does not simply exist for the purpose of producing a more efficent service, but it is the primary process by which staff are developed to the limits of individual capacity and potential. Now that the RCN has approved of a wide range of clinical, preventive and diagnostic duties as a legitimate part of the practice nurse's role (after training), it is time for primary care staff and nurse management to analyse local barriers to changes in roles and to initiate workshops and discussions on an individual basis in order to promote attitude change and changes in practice.

References

Bates B (1970) Doctor and nurse: changing roles and relationships. *New England Journal of Medicine*, **283**, 133

Bessman A (1974) Comparisons of medical care in nurse clinician and physician clinics in medical school affiliated hospitals. *Journal of Chronic Diseases*, **27**, 115–125

Bond J, Cartlidge A, Gregson B *et al* (1985) *A Study of Interprofessional Collaboration in Primary Health Care Organisations*. Report Number 27. University of Newcastle upon Tyne Health Care Research Unit

Bowling A (1981)*Delegation in General Practice. A Study of Doctors and Nurses*. London: Tavistock Publications

Bowling A (1985a) Delegation and substitution. In Harrison A & Gretton J (eds) *Health Care UK*. London: Chartered Institute for Public Finance and Accountancy

Bowling A (1985b) District health authority policy and the extended clinical role of the nurse in primary health care. *Journal of Advanced Nursing*, **10**, 443–454

Bowling A (1987a) Practice nurses – the future role. *Nursing Times*, **83**, 31–33

Bowling A (1987b) Emergence of the facilitator. *Primary Health Care*, **5**, 12–13

Bullough B (1976) Influences on role expansion. *American Journal of Nursing*, **76**, 1476–1481

Cintron G, Bigas C & Linares E (1983) Nurse practitioner role in chronic congestive heart failure clinic: in-hospital time, costs, patient satisfaction. *Heart Lung*, **12**, 237–240

Department of Health and Social Security (1977) *The Extending Role of the Clinical Nurse. Legal Implications and Training Requirements*. Health circular (77)22

Department of Health and Social Security (1986) *Neighbourhood Nursing. A Focus for Care. Report of the Community Nursing Review (Cumberlege Report)*. London: HMSO

Diers D (1982) Between science and humanity. *Yale Alumni Magazine*, **65**, 8–12

Diers D & Molde S (1983) Nurses in primary care: the new gatekeepers? *American Journal of Nursing*, **83**, 742–745

Flyn B (1974) The effectiveness of nurse clinician's service delivery. *American Journal of Public Health*, **64**, 604–611

Fullard E, Fowler G & Gray M (1984) Facilitating prevention in primary care. *British Medical Journal*, **289**, 1585–1587

Gerdes J W (1980) Geriatric nurse practitioners. *Nurse Practitioner*, **5**, 61

Golden A S (1979) The impact of new health professionals. In *National League for Nursing. Health Care in the 1980s. Who Provides, Who Plans?* New York: National League of Nursing

Goodworth C T (1985) *Effective Delegation*. London: Business Books

Greenfield S, Stilwell B & Drury M (1987) Practice nurses: social and occupational characteristics. *Journal of the Royal College of General Practitioners*, **37**, 341–345

Hasler J C, Hemphill P M R, Stewart T I *et al* (1968) Development of the nursing section of the community health team. *British Medical Journal*, **iii**, 734–736

Hodgkin G K H (1967) Saving a doctor's time with a practice nurse In Kuenssberg F V (ed) *Conference report: the Team. Family Health Care*. London: Royal College of General Practitioners

Kuenssberg E V (1971) General practice through the looking glass.*The Practitioner*, **206**, 129–145

Leitch C & Sullivan Mitchell M A (1977) State by state report: the legal accommodation of nurses practising in expanded roles. *Nurse Practitioner*, **2**, 19–30

MaGuire J (1980) *The Expanded Role of the Nurse* London: King Edward's Hospital Fund for London

Manisoff M (1979) Impact of family planning nurse practitioners. *Obstetric and Gynaecology Nursing*, **8**, 73–77

Mauksch I G (1978) Critical issues of the nurse practitioner movement. *Nurse Practitioner*, **15**, 35–36

Mauksch I G (1981) Nurse–physician collaboration: a changing relationship. *Journal of Nursing Administration*, June, 35–38

Medical Defence Union (1970) *Annual Report*. London: Medical Defence Union

Mezey, M D & McGivern D O (1986) *Nurses, Nurse Practitioners: The Evaluation of Primary Care*. Boston: Little, Brown

Molde S & Diers D (1985) Nurse practitioner research: selected literature review and research agenda. *Nursing Research*, **34**, 362–366

Nightingale F (1893) Sick nursing and health nursing. In: *Hospitals, dispensaries and nursing. Papers of International Congress of Charities, Correction and Philanthropy, Chicago, June 17th*. Billings J S & Hurd H M (eds) Baltimore: Johns Hopkins Press

Pesznecker B L & Draye M A (1978) Family nurse practitioners in primary care, a study of practice and patients. *American Journal of Public Health*, **68**, 977-980

Queen's Institute of District Nursing (1970) *Nursing in the Community*. London: Queen's Institute of District Nursing

Ramsay J A, Mendenhall R C, Neville R E (1980) Professional activities of nurse practitioners in adult ambulatory care settings. *Nurse Practitioner*, **5**, 61

Reedy B L E C (1972) Organisation and management: the general practice nurse. *Update*, **5**, 75–78, 187–193, 366–370, 433–438, 571–576

Reedy B L E C, Metcalfe A V, de Roumanie M, & Newell D J (1980) A comparison of the activities and opinions of attached and employed nurses in general practice. *Journal of the Royal College of General Practitioners*, **30**, 483–489

Report of the Royal Commission on the National Health Service. Merrison Report (1979) London: HMSO

Royal College of General Practitioners (1968) *The Practice Nurse. Reports from General Practice X*. London: Royal College of General Practitioners

Royal College of General Practitioners (1987) *Response to Neighbourhood Nursing. A Focus for Care. Report of the Community Nursing Review in England*. London: Royal College of General Practitioners

Royal College of Nursing (1977) *Evidence to the Royal Commission on the National Health Service*. London: Royal College of Nursing

Royal College of Nursing (1979) *The Extended Role of the Clinical Nurse*. London: Royal College of Nursing

Royal College of Nursing (1984) *Training Needs of Practice Nurses. Report of the Steering Group*. London: Royal College of Nursing

Royal College of Nursing (1985) *Written evidence to the Committee of Enquiry of Nursing (Cumberlege Report)*. London: Royal College of Nursing

Royal College of Nursing (1987) *RCN Response to the Consultation on Primary Health Care Initiated by the UK Health Departments*. London: Royal College of Nursing

Spitzer W O (1984) The nurse practitioner revisited: slow death of a good idea (editorial). *New England Journal of Medicine*, **310**, 1049–1051

Spitzer W O, Sackett D L, Sibley J C, *et al* (1974) The Burlington randomised trial of the nurse practitioner. *New England Journal of Medicine*, **290**, 251–256

Storms D M (1973) *Training for Nurse Practitioners: A Clinical and Statistical Analysis*. North Haven: Connecticut Health Services Research Series No. 4

Storms D M & Fox J G (1979) The public's view of physician's assistants and nurse practitioners. *Medical Care*, **5**, 526–536

United Kingdom Central Council for Nursing, Midwifery and Health Visiting (UKCC) (1986) *Project 2000: A New Preparation for Practice*. London: UKCC

Watson Hawkins J B & Thibodeau J A (1983) *The Nurse Practitioner: Current Practice*

Issues. New York: Tiresias Press

Wilson Barnett J (1986) Ethical dilemmas in nursing. *Journal of Medical Ethics*, **3**, 123–126

Woodham-Smith C (1951) *Florence Nightingale 1820–1910* New York: McGraw Hill

World Health Organization (1985) *Targets for Health for All 2000*. Copenhagen: World Health Organization Regional Office for Europe

3
Official Policies on the Extending Role of the Nurse in Primary Care in the UK – the DHSS, the Cumberlege Report and Subsequent Responses

ANN BOWLING

Attitudes towards the changing role of the practice nurse in primary health care in the UK are described in Chapter 2, and there appears to be an increasing overlapping of this role with that of the nurse practitioner in the USA. To what extent has this development been encouraged by DHSS policy?

Department of Health and Social Security Policy

The DHSS adopted a favourable stance towards extended nurse roles as long ago as 1966 when general practitioners' terms of service were rewritten to enable them to 'delegate' tasks to nurses. The changes in their terms of service also enabled them to be reimbursed for 70% of the salary of ancillary staff, including practice nurses.

Further legal changes occurred in 1968 when the Health Services and Public Health Act extended the sphere of action of health authority employed nurses from patients' homes into surgeries and clinics. Then, in 1972, GPs' terms of service were again extended to cover 'delegation' to health authority employed nursing staff. Thus there are no legal constraints to the transfer of clinical or diagnostic tasks from doctors to nursing staff.

These changes were part of a whole pattern of developments in general practice as a result of the Doctors' Charter of the mid-1960s which resulted from increasing dissatisfaction of GPs with their conditions of work and contracts of employment within the NHS: mass resignations were being threatened unless their conditions were improved (Bowling, 1981). The changes leading to incentives to employ nurses and transfer medical tasks to them were part of these developments.

The major structural changes in general practice which form the background to extended nurse roles, were:

1   The change to group practice: by 1977, 60% of GPs were working in practices of three or more doctors and, by 1984, 71% were practising in this way. This is in contrast to the single-handed and partnership practices of two which had previously been the norm.

2   The building and use of health centres: by 1977 20% of GPs were working in them and by 1984 the figure was over 25% (the number of health centres in England is now over 1 000 and in Wales has almost reached 100).

3   The development of the primary health care team with the attachment in particular of district nurses and health visitors; and, occasionally, social workers, community psychiatric nurses, psychologists and counsellors. Around 70% of district nurses and health visitors are attached to general practitioners' surgeries, rather than being attached to a geographical area (although in urban districts there is a trend back towards being area based to save nurses' travelling time where GPs' patient catchment areas are wide and overlapping).

It was the trend towards doctors practising in groups that made their own employment of non-medical staff and the attachment of health authority employed nursing staff more economical.

However, about 30% of GPs still practise alone or with only one other doctor, and the trend is towards practice in small rather than large groups of doctors. This is more common in urban areas, where there are also many problems with inadequate premises (in terms of size and facilities). Also, only one GP in four has even a part-time practice nurse (see Chapter 2). In recognition of these remaining structural barriers to professional collaboration the *Acheson Report on Primary Care* indicated that the DHSS should more actively encourage teamwork in primary care (London Health Care Planning Consortium, 1981). Partly as a result of this, Family Practitioner Committees, who administer GPs' services, were given the power in 1985, by the DHSS, to inspect premises and, if these fail to satisfy certain minimum criteria, withhold rent and rates rebates. The extent of the action taken by FPCs remains to be seen.

Guidelines on extended roles

The problem of inadequate premises apart, there has been much dispute about what tasks doctors should be permitted to transfer to nurses. The vast increase in the numbers of GP-employed practice nurses indicates that attitudes are more positive now than they were five years ago. However, confusion over appropriate roles and the legal situation has been widespread. A joint Report by the Royal College of Nursing and the Royal College of General Practitioners (1974) pointed out:

> 'In the first place it is important to know that there are *no* statutory regulations which say what a nurse can or cannot do or place an embargo on specified activities.'

As a consequence of this lack of procedure there are differences of opinion about what types of extended nurse roles are appropriate. This leads to roles that differ from surgery to surgery and from district to district (in the case of health authority employed treatment room nurses in health centres and district nurses who may work some surgery sessions) (see Chapter 2).

'Delegation' is judged to be acceptable by the DHSS only if the conditions listed in Table 3.1 below are met. There are no DHSS guidelines relating to individual tasks, with the exception of immunisations and vaccinations in 1971 and 1976.

Table 3.1   DHSS (1977) guidelines for approval of delegated tasks

- The nurse has been trained for the performance of the task and agrees to undertake it
- This training is recognised by the professions involved and the employing authorities
- The professions recognise that the task is suitable for delegation
- Delegation is practised within the context of a clearly defined policy, based on discussion and agreement by those reponsible for providing medical and nursing services

Although the DHSS has issued these guidelines, there is no official policy that more actively encourages task transference from doctors to nurses (apart from the earlier inclusion of nurses in the ancillary staff reimbursement scheme and the removal of legal barriers to task transference). The DHSS recommended that task transfer should be practised within the context of a clearly defined policy at local levels, and that discussion of what is acceptable should also take place locally. The DHSS has been forced, because of differing district policies for health authority employed nurses, to issue a number of guidelines on the delegation of vaccinations alone.

However, the situation is improving as a result of the DHSS's 1977 guidelines asking nurse managers in district health authorities to draw up local policies on the issue. The DHSS recommended that policies should state:

●   What tasks may be delegated
●   What training qualifications are necessary for the nurse performing the task
●   What safeguards accompany the delegation of particular tasks for the safety
of the patient

A survey in 1984 of all 192 health districts (response rate: 100%) found that 64% had drawn up such policies and listed tasks approved of for performance by nurses. However, only 9% of all districts clearly specified the required training, and 13% described in detail how tasks (e.g. vaccinations, ear syringing) should be carried out (Bowling, 1985a, 1985b).

Such policies relate only to DHA employed nurses – not to practice nurses employed by GPs. This is of concern in terms of training and clear structuring of roles because it is the latter who are most likely to be extending their roles.

The employment status of practice nurses themselves is the subject of controversy. The concept of the ancillary staff reimbursement scheme has angered many nurses striving towards a higher professional status for nursing: how can they be treated as equals by doctors if they are labelled as 'ancillaries'? Nurses are increasingly resentful of their traditional ancillary role in medical care (*ancilla* is the latin for maidservant/handmaiden, and ancillary is defined as subservient/subordinate to) (Gillon, 1986). Many mainstream members of the nursing profession believe it is not in the interests of nursing for some of its members to be employed by another professional group (doctors). Concern has been expressed also about the quality of the instruction some GPs give nurses who perform procedures such as cervical cytology. In particular, some members of the nursing profession have argued that it is unfair for GPs to be paid a fee for a procedure when it is the nurse who performs it (in the case of item-for-service tasks such as cervical smears and immunisations/vaccinations). This debate has been brought to the forefront recently by the *Cumberlege Report on Community Nursing* (Department of Health and Social Security, 1986a). This review body was established by the DHSS to investigate the quality, efficiency and cost effectiveness of community nursing.

The Cumberlege Report

The Cumberlege Review Body gave some thought to the roles of the practice nurse and the nurse practitioner. They recommended that GPs should no longer be reimbursed 70% of the salary of the practice nurse, and, in effect, suggested the phasing out of nurses employed by GPs. The Review Body argued that the employment of nurses by GPs led to a separate and fragmented workforce, and that it was unfair for the NHS to pay twice for 'item for service' tasks when performed by nurses (by virtue of reimbursement of 70% of the nurse's salary and the fee for item-for-service tasks).

The Report suggested instead that a proportion of family practitioner committee funds should be transferred to the community nursing services budget to enable the latter to employ, allocate and manage practice nurses within the community nursing team. It also recommended the introduction of nurse practitioners, modelled on the USA concept who, together with practice-based and community nurses, would form part of a neighbourhood-based nursing team.

The recommendations were unclear beyond this point. The report suggested that the nurse practitioner service should be provided on the basis of a set number of clinic sessions each week to be undertaken by whichever community nurse was qualified to perform the role. This, it was argued, would enable all community nurses to receive and deal with referrals direct from the public. The report therefore recommended that 'the principle should be adopted of introducing the nurse practitioner into primary health care', while on the same page rejecting a nurse practitioner grade. It was stated that any community nurse with the appropriate qualifications might perform this role. The 'appropriate qualifications', and tasks for which the nurse would qualify, were not specified (but were presumably the 'post-basic' and 'advanced' courses referred to in the recommendations).

The report also failed to clarify whether the practice nurse's role within the community nursing team would fall within that of the new nurse practitioner. The implication was that these are distinct roles, but ones that may be combined with a home visiting role. The Royal College of Nursing (1987), in its reply to the Cumberlege Report, has confirmed its view that the roles of nurse practitioner and practice nurse should be distinct, but added that trained practice nurses have the potential to develop their role into that of a nurse practitioner through 'appropriate training and qualification'.

One conclusion that can be drawn at this stage is that a more detailed analysis of the content of the practice nurse's workload is required before a separate nurse practitioner role is developed, otherwise, there is a danger of role overlap, wasteful duplication of skill and conflict between these two groups of nurses. Notice should also be taken of Greenfield et al's (1987) finding, based on their survey of practice nurses in the West Midlands, that 80% of respondents were satisfied with their current role, although many (69%) felt they were already acting in extended roles. They found that 15% wanted to expand their roles further and a few, just over 10%, wanted to give up traditional nursing tasks such as ear syringing, injections and suture removal. The need for some national figures on these issues is evident from the contrasting figures presented by Cater and Hawthorn (Chapter 9). They found, on the basis of their survey of nurses in Nottinghamshire, that far more, 39%, of practice, treatment room and district nurses wanted to extend their role in the direction of a nurse practitioner. However, less than one-third felt they had made progress in this direction.

The RCN sympathised with the Cumberlege Report's recommendations, not just over the employment structure of practice nurses and nurse practitioners, but on phasing out GPs' reimbursements (and therefore GP employed nurses) (Royal College of Nursing, 1985, 1987). These recommendations have inevitably angered many practice nurses and doctors. The government's document on primary health care (published on the same day as the Cumberlege Report), while expressing interest in the concept of a nurse practitioner, rejected the suggestions of phasing out item for service payments and the 70% staff reimbursement to GPs (Department of Health and Social Security, 1986b).

The British Medical Association's General Medical Services Committee has produced its own document in which it reacts, largely negatively, to the two goverment reports (General Medical Services Committee, 1986). Particular criticism was raised against the concept of neighbourhood-based, rather than surgery-based, nursing teams and against the recommendation to phase out GPs' reimbursements for staff (nurses) and item-for-service tasks. At the same time, the GMSC Chairman wrote to all GPs, and to their practice nurses, enclosing a copy of his committee's report, and urging them to make their views about the Cumberlege report known to the government.

The threatened practice nurses also made their voices heard in the press and in individual threats to resign from the RCN and set up an alternative professional body within the Royal College of General Practitioners (Barnes, 1986). Others have joined the Medical Defence Union (MDU) as an alternative to the RCN . For an initial annual subscription of £15, practice nurses employed by GPs can join the MDU: once accepted, the MDU offers them indemnity in all fields of their professional practice from which litigation may arise.

This has placed the RCN in a difficult position. It owes loyalty to its members who are GP employed yet is, in effect, supporting the termination of their employment. Although the Cumberlege proposals envisaged the employment of practice nurses within the community nursing service, it made no provision for priority for these posts to be given to nurses previously employed by GPs. This was partly due to criticisms voiced about their training. The ethical considerations of making over 4 000 practice nurses unemployed were not raised.

The Select Committee published its report on primary health care almost a year after the two previous DHSS reports (Department of Health and Social Security, 1986a, 1986b, 1987). It commented that nurse practitioners, working closely with general practitioners, could provide a valuable service – but only discussed them in relation to the elderly. It firmly rejected the Cumberlege Team's recommendations for changes in the employment structure of nurses and for abolition of item-for-service fees.

The Select Committee's recommendation on nurse practitioners soley for the elderly was unexpected. Its recommendations for increasing the supply of doctors to improve the quality of primary health care have, in addition, further angered the nursing profession (Fawcett-Henesy, 1987). By increasing the number of doctors it was apparently hoped that the following services would be improved:

- Family planning
- Cervical cytology
- Antenatal and postnatal care
- Vaccination
- Early detection of hypertension
- Prevention of coronary heart disease (by advice on smoking, diet and exercise)
- Prevention of mental illness
- Prevention of incapacity in the elderly

As Fawcett-Henesy (1987) has argued, nurses are undertaking this work at present, and apparently performing it at least as effectively as doctors. They are also undertaking much of the other medical work referred to in the report: management of chronic conditions such as epilepsy, asthma, diabetes, drug compliance, developmental paediatric screening, health maintenance/education and counselling. Fawcett-Henesy argued that it is apparent that the report did not start by investigating consumer needs and wants and make recommendations accordingly. The Marplan survey commissioned by the Cumberlege Review Body reported public demand for an extended nurse role in primary care and for direct public access to the services of a nurse in the surgery. Two thirds of the sample said they would be prepared to see or talk to a nurse instead of a doctor, and 60% said they would actually prefer to see a nurse for certain purposes (Department of Health and Social Security, 1986a). The Select Committee report appeared to be biased in favour of the medical profession, at the expense of nursing. This is not unusual. The Royal Commission on the NHS, reporting in 1979, followed the British Medical Association's advice, and rejected the concept of nurse practitioners (Merrison Report, 1979; British Medical Association, 1977). This was despite a review of the literature on nurse practitioners, commissioned by the Royal Commission, which was positive in its conclusions (MacGuire, 1980).

Reactions of the Royal College of Nursing

Chapter 2 describes how the Royal College of Nursing has only recently adopted an official policy favouring the introduction of nurse practitioners. In the past, the RCN has stipulated that 'delegated' medical tasks may be performed by nurses if this is not detrimental to nursing and if such duties are not regarded as the most important functions of the nurse (Royal College of Nursing, 1977, 1979). Previously, the concept was threatening to emerging nurse autonomy and professionalisation: this was because nurse practitioners had the image of being cheap substitutes for doctors. Now, as in the USA, the role is seen as being attractive to nurses and as enhancing professionalisation. The role is being practised within a philosophy of nursing (caring and whole patient care) and can lead to a substantial degree of autonomy. If patients can choose to see a nurse practitioner without being referred by a doctor, the nurse's control over health care and access to care is substantially increased. Thus the RCN, in its recent evidence to the Cumberlege Committee, called for patients to be registered with practices, rather than GPs, so that patients can choose whether to see a doctor or a nurse, for the right of nurses to prescribe a limited range of items, and for the introduction of nurse practitioners, who would be directly available to patients (Royal College of Nursing, 1987).

> 'The RCN endorses the recommendation (of the Cumberlege Committee) that the nurse practitioner role should be introduced into primary health care. We believe that the title 'nurse practitioner' and the role which it describes represents and symbolises the independent contribution of nursing to primary health care. The development of this role emphasises the profession's commitment to respond to people's expressed needs by making its expertise more directly and widely available.'

The RCN saw the nurse practitioner's role as involving direct access to nursing care for the public; an assessment of the patient's problem and health needs, including physical examinations, with the aim of maintaining healthy lifestyles, providing health education and information about illness management; full autonomy and accountability for the nurse, to include responsibility for accepting and discharging patients, planning and implementing care programmes, and referral to other practitioners; the identification and treatment of common ailments and routine health checks (Royal College of Nursing, 1987).

The Royal College of General Practitioners, in its reponse to the Cumberlege Report, concluded that the future role of a nurse practitioner in the UK depended on the results of studies analysing the work of practice nurses – given that their work involves some overlap (Royal College of General Practitioners, 1987). A decade ago the notion of nurse practitioners providing health care in the UK was controversial and had been rejected as a model by the BMA (British Medical Association, 1977; Merrison Report, 1979). Currently, the medical profession is more willing to consider the viability of a nurse practitioner role in primary care.

One essential ingredient for the successful development of innovations is that the timing has to be right (see Chapter 6). It appears that the political climate within the DHSS and the medical and nursing professions is ripe for experimentation with extended nurse roles, but it remains to be seen whether members of health authorities and the professions concerned will do this.

References

Barnes G (1986) More action for community nurses. *British Medical Journal*, (letter), **293**, 567

Bowling A (1981) *Delegation in General Practice. A Study of Doctors and Nurses*. London: Tavistock Publications

Bowling A (1985a) *Delegation and substitution*. In Harrison A & Gretton J (eds) *Health Care UK*. London: Chartered Institute of Public Finance and Accountancy

Bowling A (1985b) District health authority policy and the extended clinical role of the nurse in primary health care. *Journal of Advanced Nursing*, **10**, 443–454

British Medical Association (1977) Evidence to the Royal Commission on the National Health Service. *British Medical Journal*, **i**, 314–316

Department of Health and Social Security (1971) *International Certificates of Vaccination against Smallpox and Cholera*. Health Circular 14/70

Department of Health and Social Security (1976) *Vaccination and Immunisation-Involvement of Nursing Staff*. Health circular (76) 26

Department of Health and Social security (1977) *The Extending Role of the Clinical Nurse. Legal Implications and Training Requirements*. Health circular (77) 22

Department of Health and Social Security (1986a) *Neighbourhood Nursing. A Focus for Care. Report of the Community Nursing Review (Cumberlege Report)*. London: HMSO

Department of Health and Social Security (1986b) *Primary Health Care. An Agenda for Discussion*. London: HMSO

Department of Health and Social Security (1987) *Primary Health Care*. Social Services Committee (1st Report) London: HMSO

Fawcett-Henesy A (1987) The nursing perspective. *Update*, February 1, 278–284.

General Medical Services Committee (1986) *Report to the Special Conference of*

Representatives of Local Medical Committees. London: British Medical Association, General Medical Services Committee

Gillon R (1986) Nursing ethics and medical ethics (editorial). *Journal of Medical Ethics*, **12**, 115–122

Greenfield S, Stilwell B & Drury M (1987) Practice nurses: social and occupational characteristics. *Journal of the Royal College of General Practitioners*, **37**, 341–345

London Health Care Planning Consortium (1981) *Primary Care in Inner London* (Acheson Report). London: London Health Care Planning Consortium

MaGuire J (1980) *The Expanded Role of the Nurse*. London: King Edward's Hospital Fund for London

Merrison Report (1979) *Report of the Royal Commission on the National Health Service*. London: HMSO

Royal College of General Practitioners (1987) *Response to Neighbourhood nursing. A Focus for Care. Report of the Community Nursing Review in England*. London: Royal College of General Practitioners

Royal College of Nursing and Royal College of General Practitioners (1974) *Report of the Joint Working Party on Nursing in General Practice in the Reorganised National Health Service*. London: Royal College of Nursing

Royal College of Nursing (1977) *Evidence to the Royal Commission on the National Health Service*. London: Royal College of Nursing

Royal College of Nursing (1979) *The Extended Role of the Clinical Nurse*. London: Royal College of Nursing

Royal College of Nursing (1985) *Written Evidence to the Committee of Enquiry of Nursing (Cumberlege Report)*. London: Royal College of Nursing

Royal College of Nursing (1987) *RCN Response to the Consultation on Primary Health Care initiated by the UK Health Departments*. London: Royal College of Nursing

4
The Implications of the Cumberlege Report for the Development of a Nurse Practitioner Role

ANTHONY J CARR

Introduction

One of the recommendations of the Community Nursing Review Report (Department of Health and Social Security, 1986a) which has caused increasing interest is the proposal for a gradual introduction of the family nurse practitioner into the British community health care scene. Although the phrase 'nurse practitioner' is used in the Report it may be better to use the title 'family nurse practitioner'. This appeared to be a better descriptive title of the role of the nurse during presentations of the report, by the author, to doctors and community nurses during a tour of England in 1986. It indicates that there is an important involvement with families rather than identification with either the role of the community nurse or the medical practitioner. Both these latter roles have connotations of treating individual patients rather than families as a real purpose.

Medical and nursing roles

The traditional role of the nursing and medical professions in patient care needs a brief examination. The term 'patient' is used deliberately because in the minds of many professionals it is a 'patient' who needs care, not necessarily a person or family. One dictionary definition of patient is 'one under medical or surgical treatment.., a physician's client'. While a 'person' is described as 'a living soul or self conscious being: a personality, a human being'.

I put forward for consideration the view that one major focus of health care provision – apart from health visiting – is the offering of expert care in terms of 'a patient needing treatment'. On the other hand, many observers would prefer to see health professionals as providers of care for the whole person and the family.

The public, and some doctors and nurses, see the professions of medicine and nursing as having two separate yet at times complementary roles: namely that doctors diagnose illness, prescribe and treat the appropriate disease and the nurse then cares for the person so diagnosed. Included in that caring role is the carrying out of the doctor's medical orders. Therefore these two roles are seen as the separate ones of 'treating' and 'caring'. History confirms this image. When most people think of Florence Nightingale they think of the organisation of caring. When they contemplate great physicians of the past they consider men who have through scientific thought and application produced detailed descriptions of disease and treatment. The two roles we see are mainly 'the science of medicine' and 'the art of nursing'. To protect these roles we often hear that a caring attitude is more important in a nurse than the number of A levels she has acquired. Some would like to take the argument further and imply that a higher education may actually disqualify a person from being a nurse. The mind getting in the way of caring?

This is illustrated by criticism from nurses who look at colleagues in intensive care, renal dialysis units and operating theatres. They often state that they are more like machine minders than nurses, indicating that the caring role, and the development of relationships with patients, is of higher priority than actually treating illness. The aim of the family nurse practitioner role would be to combine these two aspects and focus on the family.

Confusion of roles: practice nurse vis-à-vis nurse practitioner

I intend to discuss here the recommendation of the Community Nursing Review Team to introduce the role of the family nurse practitioner (Department of Health and Social Security, 1986a). There can be much misunderstanding about the role of the family nurse practitioner, particularly between practice nurses and general practitioners. A personal test with the reader may help to clarify the confusion surrounding the role of the practice nurse vis-à-vis the family nurse practitioner. Given below is a list of duties for a nurse working with a general practitioner. See if these duties can be identified as being primarily the major responsibility of a practice nurse or family nurse practitioner.

● Taking a specimen of blood
● Treating a patient by prior appointment for a weekly injection or change of dressing
● Giving a variety of injections or dressings on an immediate basis in the treatment room on referral
● The removal of sutures

- Ear syringing
- Taking of ear, nose and throat swabs
- Taking specimens of sputum, faeces and urine
- Carrying out ECG recordings and operating a peak flow meter
- Immunisation and vaccination

How are these duties identified? Are they the duties of a practice nurse or family nurse practitioner? All the duties listed, and many more, are the province of the practice nurse for as long as she/he is fully prepared and tested as proficient to carry out these duties. They are all task orientated, and many registered and some enrolled nurses could be trained to undertake these tasks.

The work of a family nurse practitioner may include some of these duties if it aids her in her major role, but it is much more broadly based than doing a series of tasks. Many general practitioners and practice nurses perceive the latter's role in terms of tasks to be performed on patients. The practice nurse majors on use of skills, whereas the nurse practitioner works from a knowledge base using acquired skills and developing positive attitudes.

Preparation of the family nurse practitioner

The difference between the practice nurse and the family nurse practitioner is clearly shown by listing the aims of the educational and training programme of a family nurse practitioner in America. The aim of the training programme has been described by Conant (1970) as:

> 'A family nurse practitioner... is prepared to make independent judgements and to assume principal responsibility for primary health care of individuals and families in organised services. She assumes major professional responsibility for decision making in relation to health needs. She works collectively with physicians and other members of the health team in the delivery of health services to individuals and families. Her practice is community oriented, relates to needs, concerns, and priorities of the consumers.'

It is particularly important to note that the role relates to needs, concerns and priorities of consumers. It is not only diagnosing and treating illness, although it may include these in achieving those particular aims.

Medical and nursing educators at universities and colleges in the USA expect a family nurse practitioner, on completion of the educational programme, to be able to:

1 Identify the health or illness of an individual by taking a detailed health history, undertaking a physical examination and commencing appropriate preventive, screening and diagnostic procedures;
2 Take responsibility for the management of health and related problems of the individual with appropriate intervention measures;
3 Take responsibility for the continuing health maintenance and clinical management of stable chronically ill patients;

4   Identify the need for continuity of care for individuals and families and coordinate the evaluation, consultation and referral aspect;
5   Provide relevant health education, counselling and guidance to individuals and families;
6   Relate the individual and family health problems to the neighbourhood; identify emerging health problems and inform health planners, and help initiate appropriate intervention through community action. In terms of the Report of the Review Team this is neighbourhood nurse planning.

Conant (1970) continued his discussion of the family nurse practitioner by saying that she would have responsibility for the following:

Wellness
1   Health maintenance of all age groups – provision of continuing care to assist the patient and/or family to function at their individual optimum level of wellness.
2   Prevention:
    ● Instituting known procedures to prevent illness
    ● Screening procedures for purposes of early detection, primary prevention, health counselling and appropriate referral
    ● Health teaching and counselling of patients and families related to need and interest
    ● Periodic examination of well infants, children and adults

Illness
1   An initial assessment and evaluation of health status of the patient with needed diagnostic procedures to enable the family nurse practitioner to make one of three decisions for the care of the patient:
    ● Immediate intervention with or without medical consultation
    ● Arrangement for emergency care
    ● Referral of patient to physician
2   Provision of ongoing health maintenance and clinical management of stable chronically ill patients.
3   Identification of the impact of the health status on the individual and family in order to:
    ● Help the patient and/or family cope with the situation
    ● Plan for continuity of care

Role of the family nurse practitioner

The primary emphasis of the family nurse practitioner's role is prevention: finding out the optimum of the family's level of wellness. We may accept the importance of this concept in England, but so often our performance indicators relating to deaths from heart disease, long term disabling lung conditions,immunisation and vaccination uptakes all show that there is a long way to go before we can say that prevention is our first priority.

Screening programmes for preventive health care are ideally suited for the family nurse practitioner based in general practice: as these offer either opportunistic screening in the practice as patients consult, or selective case finding and screening of specific age groupings and potential 'at risk' groups.

Another advantage of family nurse practitioners is that they may see self-referred patients who present with the symptoms of an impending illness. In this situation preventive care and health education can be offered as an additional service and patients, having initiated the contact (and therefore exercised choice), may be more responsive. In contrast, health visitors can meet either apathy or rejection if the immediacy of the illness and the need to make a professional contact is absent.

An important feature of this new role is relationship building, which is important in developing a strategy for family care. It is more than knowing the name of the various agencies that can offer help to families in crisis – it is being that supportive person, or at least a strong link in that chain of care and support, that will be needed by some families.

A change is occurring in the concept of nursing care as district nurses and health visitors have adopted the nursing process in their approach to delivering health care. Many are now required to make a diagnosis of need and systematically to indicate a written plan of care. At the same time they are required to introduce an evaluation of that programme, making changes as necessary, and at the end give a verdict on their care, and on others associated with the programme, in order to learn from that exercise. Equally important is the integration of the family and other carers into this plan of care. This means that nurses have moved away from uninvolvement in formal diagnosis to systematic identification of the varying needs of patients. However, progress is slow.

The Team also found evidence that the chronically sick person was given a lower priority than an acutely ill person in both hospital and community settings. Evidence of considerable rigidity in nursing roles was also apparent. This is why the team proposed joint training and education for all nurses working in the community. They saw district nurses struggling with large lists of elderly chronic sick patients on continuing repeat prescription regimens. Some patients had been on the same medication for years. Health care professionals, having received most of their training in acute care settings, have been socialised into feeling that their time is better spent treating and caring for children and the acutely ill. In countries where family nurse practitioners are employed, the health status of the chronically sick patient has changed. The repeat prescription syndrome has given way to a more sensitive monitoring of the person as an individual.

The evidence presented to the Team about the limitations of current professional roles gave impetus to the recommendation to introduce the family nurse practitioner into England. The Community Nursing Review's Report *Neighbourhood Nursing – A Focus for Care* (Department of Health and Social Security, 1986a) made the following recommendation:

> 'The principle should be adopted of introducing the 'family' nurse practitioner into primary health care.'

The key tasks identified were to interview patients and diagnose and treat specific diseases in accordance with agreed medical protocols, written in detail by the practice in which the family nurse practitioner is situated.

All patients should be able to choose to consult the family nurse practitioner. She would give counselling and nursing advice to patients who are either referred by the general practitioner or who are self-referred. In addition she would be available to conduct screening programmes among specific client and age groups, and maintain patient care programmes, particularly among the chronically sick population. She would also refer patients to general practitioners and to other members of the neighbourhood nursing services as appropriate.

Taking into account the author's perceptions of the changing roles of nurses and health visitors, and the proposed shared basic nurse education (Project 2000), how is this role to be introduced into the community and who would carry it out?

Changing role of existing community nurses

The nursing profession's 'Project 2000' proposes that all future nurses would be educated, trained and registered as a 'Registered Practitioner'. Although specialisation will continue, the basic training will be different (United Kingdom Central Council for Nursing, Midwifery and Health Visiting, 1986). A considerable part of the preparation of the new nurse will be in terms of a family and community approach: this is currently lacking in basic nurse training. District nurse and health visitor training does attempt, often successfully, to wean the nurse away from a totally patient-centred approach to one of the needs of the family and community involvement. Unfortunately, much of medical training is still almost totally patient centred.

The family nurse practitioner in general practice could become a catalyst for a family-centred approach, leading to the caring for the whole person, physically, emotionally, spiritually and socially. If medicine wishes to continue to centre scientifically on the patient and the illness, what better complimentary service to offer the family than a family nurse practitioner working alongside GPs?

Who will be able to perform as family nurse practitioners? I suggest that they will be people who have taken a formal educational and training programme in this subject. Therefore practice nurses, district nurses, health visitors and school nurses should be able to choose to undertake such training and become family nurse practitioners. The family nurse practitioner may be full or part time. The advantage of a part-time appointment would be that the other half of the time could be spent actually in the community working as a nurse or health visitor. This removes the possibility of being surgery bound or developing a limited view of health and illness as presented daily in the surgery.

It will be important for family nurse practitioners to work in close collaboration with general practitioners, and work according to medically agreed protocols for that part of their work relating to diagnosis, prescription and treatment. They will work primarily from health centres and doctors' surgeries, and they will visit patients' homes to give advice and for the maintenance of health care programmes.

Basic information is needed in order to plan for the implementation of the role. How many family nurse practitioners will there be in a neighbourhood nursing team? The numbers will partly depend on how the professions, health authorities and DHSS react to this proposed role. A start could be made by looking at the average practice population. Although there is no such thing as an 'average' population the concept (see Table 4.1) gives some basic guidance. The average doctor's list is around 2000 patients (Department of Health and Social Security, 1986b). This produces the hypothetical list shown in Table 4.1, which shows the average population predicted for England as at 1988 by age group: these are then allocated to GPs on the basis of 2000 patients per doctor.

Table 4.1 Average population by age grouping (1988 projection) allocated 1–6 general medical practitioners on the basis of 2000 patients per doctor (Population source: *OPCS Monitor*, 1985. Average doctor list source: *Primary Health Care – Agenda for Discussion*. DHSS, 1986)

| | | Number of doctors in practice | | | | | |
Age	% of population	1	2	3	4	5	6
0 – 4	6.4	128	256	384	512	640	768
5 – 14	12.3	246	492	738	934	1 230	1 476
15 – 24	15.6	312	624	936	1 248	1 560	1 872
25 – 34	14.7	294	588	882	1 176	1 470	1 764
35 – 54	24.9	498	996	1 494	1 992	2 490	2 988
55 – 64	10.4	208	416	624	832	1 040	1 248
65 – 74	8.9	178	356	534	712	890	1 068
75 – 84	5.4	108	216	324	432	540	648
85 +	1.4	28	56	84	112	140	168
	100.00	2 000	4 000	6 000	8 000	10 000	12 000

By having a live list of practice patients, it is possible to plan services for them more accurately. If the child population is above average, perhaps a family nurse practitioner would be employed mainly for that age group, making the role child-care orientated. Alternatively, if there is an above average older population with chronic illnesses, the family nurse practitioner's role may be directed towards their care. It may also be thought important that the generalist nature of the role should be protected, in the short term at least, until it is more fully developed. However they are employed and utilised, it is necessary to identify need in the practice population which a nurse, having diverse skills, could help other primary care professionals to meet.

There is other information which could be gathered to help primary care professionals to provide services which are sensitive to the needs of the practice population. Census material will show them how many single-parent families they have, or assess the unemployment rate in their area. Information on the number of households that lack basic amenities (inside WC), and on over-crowding in their area can all be obtained in this way. Census material can be provided by ward although, to protect the confidentiality of the data collected from individuals, it cannot be given for each household.

Table 4.2   Average staffing of medical practices in England, assuming all staff are attached to GPs (Source: unpublished manpower figures obtained from DHSS, 1985)

Grades of staff	Number of doctors in practice						% of total staff
	1	2	3	4	5	6	
District nurses (RN)	0.37	0.75	1.12	1.50	1.88	2.25	
Registered nurses (assist DNs)	0.07	0.15	0.22	0.30	0.37	0.45	
Enrolled nurses (EN) (dist. trained)	0.11	0.22	0.34	0.45	0.57	0.68	
Enrolled nurses (no dist. training)	0.05	0.22	0.17	0.23	0.28	0.34	
Nursing auxiliaries	0.19	0.38	0.58	0.77	0.97	1.16	
	0.79	1.61	2.43	3.25	4.07	4.88	
							46
Practice nurses	0.17	0.34	0.51	0.68	0.85	1.02	
	0.17	0.34	0.51	0.68	0.85	1.02	
							9
Health visitors	0.39	0.78	1.17	1.57	1.96	2.35	
Triple/dual qualifications	0.02	0.05	0.08	0.11	0.14	0.17	
School nurses RN	0.10	0.20	0.31	0.41	0.52	0.62	
School nurses EN	0.01	0.01	0.02	0.03	0.04	0.05	
	0.52	1.04	1.58	2.12	2.66	3.19	
							30
Community midwives	0.16	0.32	0.49	0.65	0.82	0.98	
	0.16	0.32	0.49	0.65	0.82	0.98	
							9
Other RNs	0.09	0.18	0.27	0.37	0.46	0.55	
Other ENs	0.01	0.03	0.04	0.06	0.08	0.09	
	0.10	0.21	0.31	0.43	0.54	0.64	
							6
Totals	1.74	3.52	5.32	7.13	8.94	10.71	100
Family Nurse Practitioner	0.13	0.26	0.39	0.53	0.66	0.79	

In terms of the costs of this development, Table 4.2 shows the current number of community nursing staff in England. These are divided evenly between the number of practices. As an experiment, it could be suggested that the family nurse practitioner be added on the basis of five hours per week per doctor. The cost would be approximately £1520 per annum per doctor at 1986 pay levels. This compares with the total cost of community nursing services (district nurses, practice nurses, health visitors and community midwives) of approximately £15 770. The additional cost of family nurse practitioners, then, would be an extra 9.6% of existing nursing costs.

Finally, it is important to give serious consideration to this role from the point of view of consumer choice. A privately commissioned Marplan survey by the Community Nursing Review Team showed that the public are ready for this innovation. The professions may find it worth listening to what the customer wants – or is that another debatable subject?

References

Conant L (1970) *The Nature of Nursing Tomorrow*. Image: Sigma Theta Tau National Honor Society of Nursing, 4,2.

Department of Health and Social Security (1986a). *Neighbourhood Nursing. A Focus for Care. Report of the Community Nursing Review (Cumberlege Report)*. London: HMSO

Department of Health and Social Security (1986b) *Primary Health Care. An Agenda for Discussion* London: HMSO

Office of Population Censuses and Surveys (1986) *OPCS Monitor*

United Kingdom Council for Nursing, Midwifery and Health Visiting (UKCC) (1986) *Project 2000: A New Preparation for Practice* London: UKCC

5

The Ethics of Changing Roles – Issues of Responsibility and Role Overlap

PETER TOON

Primary health care is changing: taking on new areas of concern, discarding old ones no longer felt to be valuable, and trying to find new and better ways of working (Jefferys & Sachs, 1983). Change easily leads to confusion, and there appears to be much confusion about the role nurses should play in the primary health care team. Some members of the nursing profession wish to expand the role of the nurse in primary health care to that of a 'nurse practitioner' (Stilwell, 1982), and others favour the development of prevention nurses (Fullard *et al*, 1984). Some nurses have expressed concern about unmet training needs, or fears that such changes would erode professional autonomy, interfere with the nursing process and replace the nurse's proper concern with matters that are the responsibility of doctors (*Nursing Standard*, 1985). Even the words we use are difficult: the meanings attached to terms like practice nurse, nurse practitioner, community nurse, treatment room nurse and prevention nurse are not consistent. In an attempt to reduce rather than add to this confusion, the approach in this chapter will be to try to return to first principles and ask some basic philosophical questions about the provision of primary care. I hope in this way to develop a logical basis for ideas on what the role of doctors should be, what the role of nurse should be, and how they should relate to each other.

Issues in expanding the role of the nurse

Very simply, the problems can be conceptualised in the form of three questions: What needs to be done? Who should do it? How should the work be organised? These will be discussed in turn.

What needs to be done?

There are many ways in which one could describe the task of primary health care – such as in terms of client groups or in terms of the services offered. However, dividing up the areas of activity is as good a way as any of defining what primary care is.

Patients present with problems which may or may not be classified as an illness. These require diagnosis and, perhaps, treatment and follow-up. Treatment may be subdivided into drugs, practical actions (dressing and cleaning of wounds, minor surgical procedures, and so on) and 'talking treatments'. This last broad heading covers all the things 'talking' can do from giving simple information and advice about common ailments, through support and listening, to formal counselling and psychotherapy (both analytic and behavioural).

In addition to dealing with patients' problems, many people now feel that primary health care includes health promotion. In particular, the primary health care team is the major forum for two major aspects of health promotion – screening and individual health education (Royal College of General Practitioners, 1981).

It is difficult to identify an area of primary health care that cannot be accommodated within this framework.

Who should do these tasks?

Tasks have traditionally been designated as medical or nursing activities, this division having largely been determined by historical precedent. This may, or may not, lead to the best possible service for patients. Is there a better way of distinguishing medical and nursing roles?

One logical criterion for deciding who does what might be that each activity should be performed by the person best qualified by training and experience to do it well. In practice, this does not always happen. There are several other factors that can take precedence: financial, political and interprofessional consider-ations confuse the issue and require brief consideration.

Financial constraints inevitably operate: nurses are cheaper than doctors and so, when faced with a choice, economic necessity is likely to lead planners to support the cheaper option (Knott, 1985). Almost inevitably, therefore, the response of many nurses to proposals for expanding nursing roles to incorporate traditionally medical activities is resistance, suspecting exploitation.

Also, while the community nursing budgets of district health authorities are cash limited, thereby limiting the availability of district health authority employed nurses (e.g. district nurses and health visitors), family practitioner committee budgets are open ended. This makes it far easier to expand services in the latter than the former area. Therefore, many general practitioners have supported the use of practice-employed nurses, working for the general practitioner (under the ancillary staff salaries reimbursement scheme), as the only quick and easy way of expanding patients' services in primary health care, irrespective of whether this is the best administrative arrangement. This has complicated the debate over extended nurse roles – there is role overlap not only between doctor and practice nurse, but also between practice nurse and district nurse, where both perform treatments in the surgery.

Sexual politics also continue to influence the doctor–nurse relationship. Traditionally, most doctors have been men and nurses have been women, and although sex roles are changing they can still obstruct professional relationships. The subservience of women to men was in the past mirrored by the subservience of nurses to doctors. This history unfortunately continues to shape attitudes and roles.

Finally, and not entirely separate from the last point, there is professional rivalry (Bowling, 1982). The relationship between doctors and nurses, both in hospitals and in the community, is a strange one. They are trained and usually organised separately, in parallel structures. Neither is clearly in charge yet they have to work together in overlapping roles. Neither professional can function without the other. Although they may complement each other, this overlap can also lead to conflict.

These issues are important and require consideration when formulating plans, but they are not central to the aim of the whole exercise, which is to provide the best possible service to patients, rather than to find ways to deal with interprofessional issues.

Three types of task

When dividing tasks between doctors and nurses there are logically three categories. There are things doctors are trained to do better than nurses, things nurses are trained to do better than doctors, and things for which both are equally well (or badly) prepared by their training.

In primary health care, the activities that doctors are mostly better trained in are diagnosing and prescribing. Diagnosis and basic therapeutics (prescribing) is the core of undergraduate medical education, although the practical skills of prescribing are learnt mostly after provisional registration. In contrast, the basic nursing education emphasises the learning of practical skills, and in particular the meticulous performance of procedures according to a protocol. This enables nurses to be better at procedures such as sterile dressing technique and the correct administration of medications.

'Talking' treatments, health screening, follow-up care and health education are all areas in which neither profession has received sufficient training. Although all are covered to some extent in the basic training of both professions, postgraduate training is needed in these areas for both if doctors and nurses are to fulfil the needs of contemporary primary health care.

There are deeper differences of style between the training of nurses and doctors which are also relevant here. Nursing training emphasises the following of formal procedures, and includes training in organisation. Medical training is weak in these areas, but devotes more attention to problem solving and to the epidemiology and natural history of disease. Perhaps one could hypothesise that whereas medical training concentrates on the development of divergent thinking, necessary for diagnosis, nursing cultivates a more convergent approach, required for ensuring that nursing tasks are carried out properly. This is an obvious oversimplification and must be viewed with some caution: nurses learn the basic principles of physiology and anatomy, needed for diagnostic work, and doctors learn a certain amount about practical procedures (e.g. surgery).

When applying these differences in training, and the consequent differences in knowledge, skills and attitudes, a logical continuation is that we should think of primary health care tasks in three areas: core medical tasks, core nursing tasks, and a large number of procedures which could be performed by either doctors or nurses or both in collaboration. It could be suggested that core medical tasks include diagnosis and prescribing; core nursing tasks would be practical nursing procedures, and it is in the area of the overlap that guidance is needed to determine how best to develop the nursing and the medical roles.

Note that this argument makes no mention of the word delegation. This concept, often used in discussions of practice nursing (e.g. Bowling, 1981), implies that doctors have overall ultimate responsibility, and that nurses are in a subservient role, taking over some of the doctor's responsibilities while lacking in accountability and autonomy. Neither of these assumptions is helpful. Although nurses, contrary to popular belief, are responsible for their own professional actions, doctors involved in the case can also retain responsibility for these 'delegated' actions. If the two professions are to work as equal partners the concept of delegation has to go.

For this to happen training is needed for both doctors and nurses, beyond the basic professional qualification. Some such training already exists, such as vocational training for GPs, the Health Visiting Certificate and District Nursing Certificate. More courses are currently being developed for practice nurses, and for other community nurses working in preventive and counselling care. There is a need and a demand for more training. Here general practice is a few steps ahead of nursing, because it has a strong, well developed (if confusing) set of structures for postgraduate and continuing education. Perhaps nursing can learn from general practice and avoid the ramshackle *ad hoc* growth of different structures that makes postgraduate education for GPs so complicated. Perhaps, also, doctors and nurses should stop going their own separate ways in education and training. The area of role overlap suggests there must be some training overlap. This is an area where there could be more collaboration than at present. The recent development (for example, by the Open University in 1987) of postgraduate training packages suitable for doctors and nurses is a welcome step in this direction.

How should they be organised?

It seems to follow that if doctors and nurses are to work together, each with their own special areas of concern, but also collaborating, then their structural organisation should facilitate this. At present, while general practitioners are responsible solely to their patients and to the family practitioner committee, all nurses working in the community are salaried employees. Either they work for a large and hierarchical bureaucracy – the district health authority – or they are employees of general practitioners as 'ancillary staff'.

Neither option is ideal for promoting teamwork or equal professional collaboration. The first tends to promote parallel working, with varying degrees of liason but little real sharing of care, and is arguably incompatible with individual professional autonomy. The second carries the risk of the nurse being subservient to the doctor and maintaining the 'handmaiden' relationship (Department of Health and Social Security, 1986). The existence of two employing authorities with different structures, ways of working and planning has disadvantages too: it leads to overlap and lack of coordination, and necessitates much time spent on liaison work.

There are two ways by which community nursing and general practice structures could be brought into line – a salaried service for GPs or a position of professional autonomy as independent contractors for nurses working in the surgery. The former option has often been discussed but has received little support. General practitioners enjoy the flexibility and autonomy of independent contractor status. If all community nurses were also independent contractors, it is possible that they would develop as equal partners of doctors. Accountability might be to a new community health authority, based on existing family practitioner committees, who would hold practitioners' contracts and have an overall planning and administrative role.

This is merely a suggestion on how changes could be made for a more positive working relationship between GPs and nurses. Other arrangements might prove to be more satisfactory as primary health care develops. However, it is to be hoped that the structures chosen are based not on political expediency, professional aggrandisement, or a sense of historical predestination, but on assessment of how a better service can be offered to patients.

References

Bowling A (1981) *Delegation in General Practice. A Study of Doctors and Nurses*. London: Tavistock Publications

Bowling A (1982) Professional threat. *Times Health Supplement*, **10**, 19

Department of Health and Social Security (1986) *Neighbourhood Nursing. A Focus for Care. Report of the Community Nursing Review (Cumberlege Report)*. London: HMSO

Fullard E, Fowler G & Gray M (1984) Facilitating prevention in primary care. *British Medical Journal*, **289**, 1585–1587

Jefferys M & Sachs H (1983) *Rethinking General Practice – Dilemmas in Primary Care*. London: Tavistock Publications

Knott L (1985) Case for nurse practitioners. *Pulse*, **45**, 33

Nursing Standard feature (1985) Practitioners of nursing not medicine. *Nursing Standard*, **421**, 1

Open University (1987) *Coronary Heart Disease. Reducing the Risk*. Milton Keynes: Open University

Royal College of General Practitioners (1981) *Prevention of Arterial Disease*. London: RCGP

Stilwell B (1982) The nurse practitioner at work. *Nursing Times*, **78**, 1799–180

6
Introducing Innovation – Overcoming Resistance to Change

BARBARA STOCKING

Introduction

People often embark on a programme of change without being clear about what precisely it is that they are trying to do and why. Nor are they always clear about the implications of the change for others and, therefore, what sort of resistance they are likely to meet. They are then surprised at others' reactions, disheartened by the slow progress being made, and often end by giving up. To be successful in bringing about change requires a good deal of clarity and analysis as well as energy and persistence.

In this chapter I shall try to identify the sorts of innovations that are likely to be accepted, or not; what sort of development the nurse practitioner role is in these terms; and, finally, some thoughts about bringing about change. Most of the lessons and conclusions I describe are based on a study undertaken several years ago to look at the diffusion of patient care innovations in the National Health Service (Stocking, 1985).

In this study I investigated 22 innovations, some of which had diffused widely in the NHS while others had not. Some of these mainly involved technological change, others organisational change, and some a mixture of the two. The purpose was to try to define the characteristics of innovations most likely to lead to wide diffusion. In the second part of the study four innovations were analysed in more detail in particular districts and regions in an attempt to undertand why they were accepted in one place and not in another.

57

Before describing the characteristics of successful or unsuccessful innovations it is necessary to think about the process of diffusion of innovation.

The diffusion process

New ideas have to start somewhere. Perhaps they are the result of a technological breakthrough, for example CT scanners; perhaps they merely formalise something that was already taking place, as in the development of the geriatric day hospital movement; perhaps they are adaptations of something seen overseas (the nurse practitioner is an example here); or perhaps they are a new way of meeting desperate need. Wherever they come from and for whatever reasons, there will be some individuals who have developed, or who are promoting, the idea. The extent to which these people are respected in their own fields and the energy with which they go about promoting the idea will strongly influence the uptake of the innovation. As shown in Fig. 6.1, the innovators will disseminate an idea but that does not mean that, in any particular location, those who hear about it will immediately accept it. People will need to be persuaded of its benefits and, unless it affects only their personal practice, the innovators will need to persuade others that it is an idea worth considering.

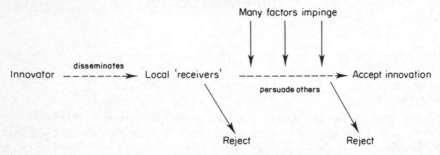

Fig 6.1   The diffusion process

At this stage, many factors will come into play: the characteristics of the innovation itself, the personalities and interests of the people concerned, and the characteristics of the local environment. These will all add up to either acceptance or rejection. Of course, this is only at one moment of time: the situation may change, and something which seemed impossible may suddenly be welcomed. For example, if the idea is taken up by others in neighbouring districts, or by the key opinion leaders, it may alter the views of those who originally resisted the idea.

Characteristics of successful innovation

What then do we know about innovations that are likely to diffuse widely? Table 6.1 summarises the factors common to successful and unsuccessful innovations, as well as highlighting characteristics that, in my particular study, did not seem to have as much influence as might have been expected.

Table 6.1   Characteristics of innovations

Successful
Climate of opinion right
Enthusiastic national and local champions
Meets desperate need
'Adds on'
Little explicit finance
Able to be adapted locally

Unsuccessful
Incompatible with roles, attitudes, routines
Complex to organise
Relatively little benefit

Factors less important than expected
Clinical trials
Finance

The climate of opinion

The first factor is the climate of opinion in society as a whole or in the NHS. The influence of changes in the climate of opinion is illustrated by two examples from my study. Regional secure units are designed to treat and rehabilitate mentally ill patients who are so dangerous or disturbed that ordinary NHS hospitals cannot be expected to contain them. In 1974, when the Department of Health and Social Security asked each region to provide secure accommodation for these people, there was considerable resistance to the idea. Psychiatric hospitals had only recently unlocked their doors and secure units were seen as a retrograde step. Ten years later the situation had completely changed. Staff had seen some of the newly built secure units, as well as some of the upgradings of existing buildings carried out to provide interim secure units. Secure units began to be seen as a prestigious development, and also one that might save a psychiatric hospital from closure. Thus there is now more interest from psychiatric hospitals in developing secure facilities.

A different example is that of the prevention of rickets in Asians. The occurrence of rickets in Asian children was first identified in Glasgow in 1962, and then subsequently found in other towns and cities. For many years there was a reluctance to start campaigns against rickets because this might be seen as a racist move, and because a prevailing view was that the Asian population should use NHS facilities and therefore no special approach was required. These attitudes towards the needs of ethnic minority groups gradually changed in the 1970s so that it became possible to run a national 'Stop Rickets' campaign in 1981.

Thus, with any innovation it is worth considering whether the time is right, or whether the climate of opinion is such that the innovation is likely to be rejected out of hand.

Product champions

It is rare for ideas to take root spontaneously. More often, committed individuals give a great deal of time and energy to getting their ideas known and accepted. This is true both for those who are trying to put an idea on the national agenda, and for those who are trying to get the change accepted locally. Because of the parallels with industry I have called these people 'product champions': they are the people who keep the idea on the agenda and devote themselves to achieving change.

This may sound as though anyone who devotes him/herself to a cause can bring about change. In fact, this is not enough. Sometimes the product champions just do not have enough power and influence in the system to have their ideas accepted. For example, if at national level the innovator is perceived as a maverick, always coming up with wild ideas, a particular innovation is unlikely to be accepted. It requires the respected opinion leaders in a particular specialty or profession to support an idea before it is likely to be widely accepted.

At local level, my study illustrated the power of different groups. One issue concerned changing the time that patients are woken up in hospital, early waking being a perennial complaint by patients. Usually, the people trying to bring about change were ward sisters, nurse managers or, occasionally, community health councils. They were successful in bringing about change in some places, but in one hospital, where the Chairman of the Medical Executive Committee was opposed to the changes, the initiative was completely blocked.

Similarly, in the Asian rickets example, one city had a high-powered campaign because it was promoted by an Asian general practitioner who was well known nationally, although at the same time there seemed to be no evidence of rickets. In another area the product champion was a community dietitian whose influence was not accepted by doctors and managers, and as a result a 'Stop Rickets' campaign was never undertaken.

Thus, it is not only necessary to have local people who are committed to an idea – they must be able to influence the groups involved in the decision. Of course, different innovations will affect different groups. A community health council may have the power base to start a Good Practices in Mental Health scheme, but is not likely to be a successful product champion of regional secure units.

Needs

An innovation is likely to be taken up quickly if it meets a desperate need. For example, reality orientation therapy for the elderly mentally ill was widely accepted because it met the needs of staff trying to do something for severely demented people. The opposite case is also true: that innovations with little perceived benefit are not likely to be accepted easily.

Patients do not necessarily have to benefit directly from the innovation. In many cases the benefits may be at least as much for staff, or reassuring to patients, rather than benefits in terms of health outcomes. Electronic fetal monitoring (EFM) is an example here. The clinical trials that assessed the outcome benefits to babies were carried out several years after the diffusion of the technology. In the early stages of diffusion, fetal monitoring seems to have been accepted because it helped both staff and patients feel secure that the baby's condition during labour was satisfactory.

The EFM example illustrates another point: that clinical trials seemed, at least in my study, to have relatively little effect on the diffusion of innovations. Innovations have usually been accepted or rejected before the results of clinical trials are available, although the results may change the use of a procedure or, if there are positive results, perhaps convert the more sceptical.

Compatibility

Probably the central characteristic that determines the acceptance or rejection of an innovation is compatibility with professional roles and attitudes, and with work routines. It is difficult to bring about change that operates against these factors. For example, nurse specialist roles have been difficult to achieve partly because nurses are not themselves sure how they fit in with traditional roles and hierarchies, and other influential groups such as doctors may be equally confused. The organisation of the in-patient day is an issue that illustrates how difficult people find disruption to routines. For example, altering patients' waking times would, on superficial analysis, seem to be a straightforward change which would improve patients' comfort. However, achieving the change involves disrupting many routines: day/night nursing staff work arrangements, cleaning schedules, meal times and, therefore, catering staff, etc. This change shows how important it is to think through the implications for other staff before promoting a particular idea.

Nevertheless, champions promoting such difficult innovations should not give up. It is possible to bring about 'incompatible' changes. It may take longer, and require more negotiation, but the advantage then is that the innovation may stick. If people have been persuaded, and are convinced about, a fairly fundamental change, rather than just giving lip service to it, it is unlikely that they will go back. The converse also seems to be true: the innovations that are easily achieved because they simply 'add on' to everything else, and are unthreatening, are also those that slip away most easily. For example, the product champion moves to a new job and the reality orientation therapy notice board soon displays the wrong date!

Complexity

Another stumbling block to change is complexity. The waking times example illustrates how a fairly simple change can often become complex. The Asian rickets example is another. Giving out vitamin D tablets to all children with, or at risk of, developing rickets does not sound too complex. Once the task is analysed it can be seen to involve a large number of different workers who need to operate in a coordinated manner: school nurses, clinical medical officers, health visitors, general practitioners, etc. Innovations that require the involvement of many different professional groups, and a great deal of organisation, are not likely to be easily accepted.

Finance

Many people believe that it is lack of money in the NHS that prevents change. In my study there was some support for this in a few cases, but the overwhelming impression was that if people really wanted to do something they could find the funds. If the innovation is an item of equipment, hospitals' Leagues of Friends or public appeals are possible. Voluntary agencies provided funds for other small-scale changes. There are ways of squeezing other resources, for example, changing the way staff spend their time, which makes an innovation possible. Some of the fastest diffusing innovations required little explicit finance, but often required a change in use of time. Although some of the very expensive innovations, such as regional secure units, required central funding before they were established, for most of the innovations the need for finance was less important than an observer of the NHS might expect.

Adaptability

The last characteristic I should like to discuss is the possibility of adapting an innovation to suit local needs. Innovators are often concerned about this issue because they feel that if the innovation is not introduced 'properly' it may then not work and the idea may fall into disrepute. On the other hand, ideas that have been fully integrated into the system may lose some of their trappings. For example, crisis intervention teams may never become widespread, although the concept of crisis intervention as an approach may become more commonly accepted.

An additional point is that if local people can put their mark on an innovation they may find it much more acceptable: regional secure units are an example. In the mid-1970s the design of secure units was established but a number of regions argued that this type of unit did not meet their needs. Over time, more variation in design was accepted and regions adopted the idea in various ways. Initially one unit per region was the accepted ratio, but some regions are now setting up much smaller units for local catchment populations.

Nurse practitioners

What does all this imply for the development of the nurse practitioner role and for practice nurses? Practice nurses appear to be well accepted because they meet a need, and because finance is available. Perhaps most of all they do not significantly threaten existing roles. Practice nurses have been 'added on' to practices and health centres, taking on some of the tasks from doctors but, in most cases, without threatening the doctor's central role as the patient's first contact and the diagnostic assessor of needs.

The nurse practitioner role is rather different because it involves nurses making first contacts with patients. If practice nurses wish to develop into nurse practitioners they will need to recognise these fundamental differences. Studies have shown that some practice nurses and attached district nurses do, at the doctor's request, have first contacts with patients (Bowling, 1981; Cartwright &

Anderson, 1981). However, this practice was not supported by their respective professional bodies until recently, because first contact is seen as central to the doctor's role. Currently, the Royal College of General Practitioners is willing to discuss first contact roles for nurses; and the Royal College of Nursing is openly in favour of such roles in view of the potentially increased status this can give to nurses and because of the expansion of patients' services that it can lead to (see Chapter 3). If the nurse practitioner role is to be fully accepted by both professions, agreement will have to be reached on whether the GP's central role is the assessment and diagnosis of all patients or whether, and in what circumstances, this role can be taken on by the nurse practitioner. There already appears to be some agreement that this role can be transferred to the nurse in certain circumstances (eg.in the case of screening for preventable conditions – see Fowler et al, Chapter 8).

One factor in the acceptability of the innovation may be its product champion in local circumstances. The practice nurse may not have enough power to convert doctors to the idea, although this may not always be the case. It is possible that the doctors themselves will champion the idea, as some have done in the past. Once some nurse practitioners are in post, and working successfully, this should persuade others, who may wish to be in the forefront of primary care developments, to accept the idea.

Despite these rather negative characteristics, there are others that support the acceptance of nurse practitioners. Although not all nurses would support the development, there is a widespread view that, in hospital and community settings, there is a need to enhance the nurse's clinical role and professional status: the nurse practitioner movement coincides with these concerns. Among doctors, too, there may be changes. Some GPs are ready to accept that patients should have a choice about which professsional they wish to see, and recognise that in the innovatory experiments nurses as first contacts have been well accepted. Some also recognise that nurse practitioners may be cost effective overall for the National Health Service, as they enable doctors to use their time more effectively. Some doctors recognise that the nurse practitioner may have more time and better counselling skills than they have, and therefore can help to provide a better service for patients. However, it has not been demonstrated in the UK that the nurse practitioner role is needed to meet any 'desperate' health care need, however this might be defined. Thus the benefits of this position will have to be defined clearly.

Whether working at a national or local level to promote the uptake of the concept of nurse practitioners, it is worthwhile analysing the characteristics of successful and unsuccessful innovations to see where the role is placed at the present time.

Bringing about change

There is no clear blueprint for bringing about change. However, there are lessons from my own study, and from others, about how change has, or has not, been achieved. Change agents should first ask themselves what they are trying to achieve, and whether the particular innovation is the best approach. In other words, a good diagnosis is required first. Sometimes innovations may be searching for application, rather than having been designed to meet identified needs. Muddled reasons for promoting an innovation are likely to meet resistance. The right timing also needs to be considered. If the climate of opinion is strongly against the innovation, unless the champion is very brave or powerful, it may be better to wait. Energy can be directed first to changing the general climate of opinion before promoting the particular innovation.

Once the product champion is convinced that the idea is good, and is clear about the reasons why, the audience (those who need persuading) will need to be identified. For some innovations in health care the number of individuals and agencies involved can be considerable (such as when setting up group homes or drop-in centres in the community for the mentally ill). Even in small organisations such as health centres there may still be a number of people to influence. The essential need is to understand why the people concerned are likely to see the innovation as beneficial or disadvantageous. Altruistically, one might hope that this personal judgement would be based on benefits to the patient.

There are many other important factors. For each person concerned the questions will include: What does this innovation do to my status in the organisation? Will it mean my work is different? Will it alter my routines? How will it be perceived by others whom I respect outside the practice? (for example, for GPs these might be other colleagues or, for some, colleagues on national bodies and committees). The individual is likely to make an intuitive or even explicit analysis of all these factors before accepting or rejecting an innovation.

The product champion needs to understand these attitudes – just because the innovation is exciting to them does not mean it would have the same benefits for other people. Where there are clear disadvantages for others some thought then needs to be given to how these might be offset. Could the innovation be part of a package whereby the 'loser' gains something else they are known to want? Sometimes people are just afraid of the unknown. It may be possible to overcome this by taking them to see the innovation in operation elsewhere, or encouraging them to talk to their peers who have had experience of it.

The issue of alliances is also important. Sometimes several different groups are, unknown to the others, trying to promote similar ideas. If there are sufficient differences between their innovations they may even inadvertently be destroying each other's ideas. Joining together may be much more powerful, even if some compromise is needed. For product champions who recognise themselves as being fairly low in the 'pecking order' (considering who needs to be influenced for the particular innovation) they may need to identify someone sympathetic to their ideas to promote them in committees or discussions when they themselves are absent.

To some readers these steps may seem obvious, but it is surprising how many people expect to bring about change without having thought carefully about who they need to influence and their strategy for doing so.

The final point concerns timing. Change can sometimes happen quickly but more often it is a long slow process. Champions will need a great deal of determination and persistence to keep the issue on the agenda, and to keep working to overcome resistance. They will also need patience with those who raise the standard British objections:

1   We've never done it before!
2   We tried it before!
3   X will not like it!
4   We haven't the time, money, staff, etc.!

and worst of all:

5   You're right but!

References

Bowling A (1981) *Delegation in General Practice. A Study of Doctors and Nurses*. London: Tavistock Publications
Cartwright A & Anderson R (1981) *General Practice Revisited. A Second Study of Patients and their Doctors*. London: Tavistock Publications
Stocking B M (1985) *Initiative and Inertia*. London: Nuffield Provincial Hospitals Trust

PART II

Nurses in Extended Roles
in the United Kingdom

7

Nurse Practitioners in British General Practice

BARBARA STILWELL   DOREEN RESTALL
BARBARA BURKE-MASTERS

In this chapter three different styles of nursing practice are described. The first is a project to evaluate the nature of the work of a nurse practitioner (Barbara Stilwell) introduced to an inner city practice in Birmingham, where research evaluating her role has been ongoing since the inception of the project. The second is a nurse practitioner (Doreen Restall) operating within a large primary care team in rural Scotland. The third (Barbara Burke-Masters) provides a service as a doctor surrogate for a section of the population who would otherwise have difficulty obtaining medical attention.

This chapter reflects different aspects of nurse practitioner role development, which have also been reported in North America.

A nurse practitioner in an inner city general practice   *Barbara Stilwell*

The early 1980s was a time ripe for change in British primary health care. The government-commissioned report on inequalities in health, chaired by Sir Douglas Black, found evidence of widening and considerable differences in both morbidity and mortality between those at the top and those at the bottom of the social scales. The report suggested:

> 'A shift in resources is not enough; it must be combined with an imaginative (and in part necessarily experimental) approach to health care and its delivery.'
> (Department of Health and Social Security, 1980)

A new approach to health care was also a timely response to the changing nature of work in general practice. In 1976 Mackichan had suggested that general practitioners' workload no longer consisted mainly of diagnosing physical illness, but more of the management of social and psychiatric problems.

Cartwright and Anderson (1981) found, in a national survey of patients and their doctors undertaken in 1977, that the proportion of consultations judged by general practitioners to be trivial or unnecessary had not changed since Cartwright's earlier 1964 survey (Cartwright, 1967). They also noted 'a clear association between the proportion of patients who thought their doctor was "not so good" about taking time and not hurrying them and the proportion of surgery consultations the doctors regarded as trivial, inappropriate or unnecessary'. Could a nurse practitioner, acting as first contact for people visiting general practitioners, differentiate between the trivial and more serious condition? More importantly, could a nurse practitioner provide opportunities for preventive procedures and health education which might improve the health status of a vulnerable practice population in the inner city?

With these questions in mind, a research project was designed to test the hypothesis that a nurse practitioner working in general practice would meet needs not met by other health care professionals without increasing hospital use. The project was supervised in the Department of General Practice at Birmingham University, where the author was a research fellow in addition to being the nurse practitioner in an inner city general practice. The project was funded within the department by the West Midlands Regional Health Authority.

The nurse practitioner's role

The role of the nurse practitioner was based on that developed in the USA (and discussed in earlier chapters). For the purpose of the project the scope of practice of the nurse practitioner was summarised as:

1   Assessing the physical and psychosocial health status of individuals and families by taking an adequate history and physical examination;
2   Discriminating between normal and abnormal physical findings;
3   Evaluating data collected to decide on treatment either independently or with a physician;
4   Managing the care of patients by protocols agreed previously with the general practitioner in the practice and the supporting medical staff of the Department of General Practice;
5   Being aware of the importance of helping the person consulting to set long-term health goals, and being sensitive to individual learning needs in relation to the health education incorporated into each consultation.

This role had obvious training implications for the nurse practitioner, who had been a hospital nurse for many years and had also worked for several years as a health visitor.

'Apprenticeship' training was planned and undertaken by the nurse practitioner. This involved being present during selected general practitioners' consultations with patients, as well as in certain consultants' clinics, to learn the

techniques of physical examination. Also included in this training were identification of common signs and symptoms, and understanding of when they were
potentially serious; management and advice of common ailments (e.g. upper
respiratory tract infection); and use of drugs and investigations in common
ailments. Protocols for the management of common disorders were agreed by the
doctors involved in the project and the nurse practitioner. These guidelines,
which set out the physical signs of certain conditions, their management and
need for referral, were based on the patient care guidelines developed at North
Carolina University by Hoole *et al* (1982).

The structure of the project

A small pilot project was undertaken in an inner city practice in Birmingham for
six months. The aim was to develop the objectives for the major study, which was
carried out in a different inner city practice in North Birmingham. The pilot
developed the study objectives as:

1   To determine whether the extended role of the nurse in the setting of
     general practice is acceptable to patients and professional colleagues;
2   To examine the motives and expectations of patients who choose to consult
     the nurse practitioner rather than the doctor;
3   To identify aspects of patient care which may be safely undertaken by the
     nurse practitioner.

The practice

The practice in which the main study took place was located in an inner city area,
north of Birmingham city centre, and adjacent to a large motorway complex.

At the beginning of the study two male doctors worked in the same building,
although they were not partners. Six months after the project began, a female
doctor joined one of these as a partner. 4 728 patients were registered with both
practices, of whom 49% were female. The nurse practitioner saw patients from
both practices and worked with all three doctors. At the beginning of the project,
patients were seen on a first-come, first-served basis, from 8 a.m. to 9 a.m. and 5
p.m. to 6 p.m. each day. Eventually the nurse practitioner's hours were changed
to 9 a.m.–12 noon and 4–7 p.m., in response to patients' requirements.

Nurse practitioner consultations

The nurse practitioner began work in the North Birmingham practice in October
1982, when the main study also began. Prior to this there had been no nurse
working in the practice, apart from a two-hour weekly session, for immunisations
and routine injections, run by the attached community nurse.

Patients were informed about the availability of the nurse practitioner for
consultations by a large notice in the waiting room, which outlined her work.
Receptionists were instructed to ask patients attending the practice, in a non-
directive manner, whether they wished to see the doctor or the nurse practitioner.

The nurse practitioner worked in a consulting room similar to that of the doctors in the practice, and did not wear a uniform. She consulted for eight half days per week, seeing eight to ten patients during each session.

Patients were offered a 20 minute appointment with the nurse practitioner. This long consultation was felt to be necessary in order to provide a full nursing assessment, time for health education, and time for patients to express their anxieties. Most patients were seen in the surgery but home visits were made if necessary. First home visits were not undertaken.

Nurse practitioner consultations were informal in structure, with both patient and nurse seated in chairs set at the corners of a table in order to enhance feelings of collaboration and equal status (Argyle, 1983). Patients were encouraged to discuss whatever concerns they had, whether physical, mental, social or emotional. This style of consultation was adopted because it was hoped that it would facilitate a closer relationship between the nurse and patient, which, as Peplau (1952) has described, crucially influences the outcomes of nursing care.

The aim of each nursing consultation was to deal with the presenting problems, taking into account factors other than physical sypmtoms, and ultimately focusing on long-term health education and anticipatory care. If patients did not spontaneously ask for advice, the nurse practitioner prompted their interest with questions such as: 'Do you smoke?' or 'When were you last weighed?' (Stilwell, 1985).

If a prescription was needed, the nurse practitioner took the notes, with a prescription written out according to agreed protocols, to the general practitioner free at the time, and it was signed. An outside observer (a GP) visiting the practice, and timing aspects of the nurse practitioner consultation, said that the process of getting a prescription signed took, on average, three minutes (Garrett, 1986, personal communication).

Data collection

Three methods of data collection were used:

1   Details of all nurse practitioner consultations were recorded on an encounter form between March and August 1983. Patients' age, sex, ethnic group and presenting problem were recorded, together with problems discussed during the consultation, any investigations requested, prescriptions given and referrals. It was not possible, for organisational reasons, to record patients' social class. Details of the social class and ethnic stucture of the total practice population were not available (however, see (2)).The RCGP-OPCS Morbidity Statistics from *General Practice Diagnostic Classification Manual* (1981) was used to classify patients' problems.

2   A randomly selected sample of 140 patients were sent postal questionnaires which asked their opinion about care from the nurse practitioner. Replies were anonymous, but respondents were asked to note their occupation, age, sex and place of birth (of selves and parents). They were asked how they felt about the introduction of a nurse practitioner into the practice, and their degree of satisfaction with any consultations with her.

3   The nurse practitioner's colleagues were sent a postal questionnaire asking about their attitudes towards her role: nine staff were questioned (doctors, receptionists, health visitors, community nurses and midwives).

The nature of the nurse practitioner's work

During March to August 1983, 858 patients consulted the nurse practitioner. Data relating to these patient contacts has been analysed and the results are presented here. Eighty-nine per cent of consultations took place at the surgery: the 858 patients presented 979 problems, and 492 additional problems were raised by 46% of the patients. Over half (54%) of the patients chose to see the nurse practitioner, rather than being referred by someone else. The majority of patients originated from the UK and one-fifth from Pakistan or the New Commonwealth: there appeared to be no special selection of nurse practitioner consultations by racial group (Table 7.1).

Table 7.1   Ethnic group of patients who consulted the nurse compared with the ward population

Ethnic group	% of ward population	% of nurse's patients
UK	92.5	73.1
Irish Republic	4.5	5.0
New Commonwealth	1.9	14.2
Pakistan	0.2	5.6
Others	0.9	0.8
Not known	—	1.3

Birmingham Inner City Profile, 1982

Table 7.2 shows the distribution of problems among the 18 diagnostic categories of the RCGP-OPCS (1981) Although patients presented with problems in all groups the majority (60%) fell into the category of Supplementary Classification. The largest proportion of these consultations (50%) were for preventive medicine, followed by advice and health education (25%), followed by social, marital/family problems and administration (e.g. referral letters, prescriptions, certificates) (20%). The nurse practitioner managed 45% of cases without prescription, referral or investigation; 19% were referred to others (usually to the GP but also to consultants and social services); 15% received a prescription. The nurse practitioner ordered 210 investigations including 153 laboratory tests and 42 cervical smears.

What did the nurse practitioner provide for patients?

The nurse practitioner acted as an alternative consultant for patients. They appeared to consult her appropriately, as an alternative to a GP, as in 45% of cases no prescription, referral or investigation was needed. No instances of the nurse practitioner failing to alert others to serious signs and symptoms were noted by any of the medical staff. Thus for many patients this style of care seems to be a safe and appropriate alternative to consulting a physician.

Table 7.2   Comparison of the distribution of patient–nurse contacts (by diagnostic group), with patient–doctor contacts in National Morbidity Survey (NMS), General Household Survey (GHS) and Nottingham Survey (NOTTS)

	Diagnostic group	No. of problems in each group	As % of all problems presented	NMS 1970/71 (%)	GHS 1971 (%)	NOTTS 1974 (%)
I	Intestinal and other infections	34	2.3	3.7	5.6	5.2
II	Neoplasms	3	0.2	1.5	0.5	1.4
III	Endocrine and metabolic	5	0.3	2.2	1.6	2.5
IV	Blood and blood-forming organs	3	0.2	1.0	1.1	0.9
V	Mental disorders	55	3.7	9.9	4.9	6.3
VI	Nervous system and sense organs	40	2.7	6.9	5.2	7.1
VII	Circulatory	7	0.5	8.5	7.5	10.9
VIII	Respiratory	53	4.3	18.9	19.6	18.8
IX	Digestive	21	1.4	5.4	6.1	4.8
X	Genitourinary	53	3.6	5.1	4.2	4.2
XI	Pregnancy	4	0.3	1.1	1.3	0.7
XII	Skin and subcutaneous tissue	34	2.3	6.5	4.2	5.6
XIII	Musculoskeletal	84	5.7	6.8	4.9	8.2
XIV XV	Congential anomalies and Perinatal diseases	2	0.1	0.1	0.4	0.2
XVI	Symptoms and ill-defined conditions	154	10.5	6.7	6.8	6.8
XVII	Accidents, poisoning and violence	30	2.0	5.3	7.4	6.0
XVIII	Prophylactic procedures	879	59.8	8.4	18.8	11.4

The number of problems that fell into the Supplementary Category 18, and were presented to or discussed with the nurse practitioner, was higher than the same category of problem presented to doctors in two other studies, compared with the nurse practitioner study in Table 7.2. This high number might reflect the length of consultations: Morrell *et al* (1986) found that general practitioners who have 10-minute consultations with patients (rather than the average 6 minutes) are more likely to advise on prevention and health education.

From the number of signs, symptoms and ill-defined conditions (Supplementary Classification 16) that patients presented to the nurse practitioner, it seems that they consulted her for advice or reassurance about vague symptoms. There is no evidence that these are the trivialities of which, in the past, general practitioners have complained (Cartwright & Anderson, 1981), but it seems likely that some of them were, and were dealt with without serious mishap by the nurse practitioner.

Allen *et al*'s analysis of 'good' primary health care nursing concludes that taking time with patients and listening to them are important components of nursing care. It was this aspect of nurse practitioner care that patients in this study valued most (see Chapter 10). It may also have been this style of care that facilitated the large numbers of patients wanting information or advice about their health and the prevention of disease. More research is needed to establish such a link.

The development of a nurse practitioner role in rural Scotland
Barbara Stilwell   Doreen Restall

Between 1980 and 1982 Doreen Restall, then a community nurse, participated in a research study which was designed to screen for and identify depression in the elderly. The interviews, which were conducted by Restall, covered physical, social and environmental aspects of health. Of the 1778 people over retirement age interviewed, 17% were reported to have some unmet need. Many attributed their physical problems to their age and others felt their problems were 'too trivial to bother the doctor with'. Restall felt that most of their problems could have been dealt with by giving simple advice, education or treatment, and people's quality of life would have been improved.

As a result of documenting this unmet need, Restall felt that the gap in care might be filled by the role of the nurse practitioner, as found in North America. She envisaged a nurse practitioner who would be freely available for patients to consult, who could manage uncomplicated problems, institute preventive measures, and provide emotional support and guidance.

Accordingly, Restall negotiated with the general practitioners, in whose practice she was attached as a community nurse, to extend her role to that of nurse practitioner. She was given a trial period in which to demonstrate the value of the role to the doctors. Training in various aspects of physical examination was given in the practice and in the local general hospital. One GP was responsible for teaching her techniques such as accurate blood pressure recording and abdominal palpation. At Aberdeen Royal Infirmary she learnt about the significance of laboratory results, and techniques of taking a cervical smear and taking and reading an electrocardiogram. Her consequent job description, drawn up by herself and the GPs she worked with, set out her objective:

'To provide an alternative consultative pattern (for) the public, particularly to meet the needs of those patients who would not normally attend the general practitioner with so-called 'trivial' or minor illnesses. The nurse practitioner's role includes assessment, problem-solving, teaching, counselling and health education. The nurse practitioner can evaluate, screen, identify and assist to identify illness and render appropriate treatment where necessary, or refer to the general practitioner.'

Doreen Restall, as a nurse practitioner, works with seven GPs and two practice nurses. The latter carry out routine nursing tasks, such as dressings and injections, as Restall does not consider these to be part of the nurse practitioner's role. The procedures that she lists as part of her job description are:

- Electrocardiogram
- Hypertension clinic
- Smears, swabs, specimens
- Skin testing
- Immunisations
- Bladder retraining programmes
- Ear syringing
- Chest examination
- Health education
- Counselling (e.g. smoking, obesity, alcohol, menopause, marital problems)

Restall is specific about her role in diagnosis, adding to her job description:

'The nurse practitioner may diagnose in some cases. She may screen for serious illness by the recognition of signs and symptoms of disease. This will include the use of tools normally used by general practitioners. The nurse practitioner must realise her limitations and refer to the general practitioner.'

She sees any patient who wishes to consult her. Occasionally a patient who attends without an appointment for doctor or nurse practitioner is asked if he/she is willing to see the nurse practitioner rather than the doctor. Any prescriptions that are needed are obtained from one of the doctors in the practice.

Although no formal research has been carried out monitoring or evaluating Restall's role, she feels that most of her work is health education and counselling. Of patients presenting with physical problems, she says most are upper respiratory tract infections, skin rashes, ear infections, backache, aches and pains in muscles, vaginal discharges, urinary tract infections, cervical smears, and concerns about lumps. If she feels a problem is beyond her competency she informs the patient and advises him/her to see the doctor, perhaps doing any necessary screening first (e.g. blood pressure recording). If she feels the problem is urgent she calls the GP into the consulting room immediately. Restall is also involved in improving the cardiovascular disease screening programme for the practice. Protocols are currently being drawn up by Restall and the GPs for such conditions as hypertension, thyroid disease and mild heart failure.

No conclusion can be reached about the impact of this role on the practice, or on the patients, without an evaluation programme, although Restall and her colleagues feel they have improved the quality of care for patients by adding a new dimension to the practice.

A nurse practitioner in a centre for homeless people with alcohol problems
Barbara Burke-Masters

The nature of the problem

In 1980, I returned home from a post working in a very extended nursing role for the Catholic medical missions in the Third World, to discover another Third

World in Britain. Homeless and destitute people, the vast majority of whom were male and with an alcohol problem, were denied proper primary health care and, therefore, other health services via the state primary health care system. Numerous studies, from 1970 onwards, have shown that homeless people not only suffer high levels of illness and handicap, but are also likely to have greater difficulty in gaining access to health services. Difficulties have repeatedly been reported from many areas in finding GPs willing to provide health care for homeless people, even as temporary patients. In effect, thousands of people living rough or in hostels have no access to a local doctor (Griffiths, 1981). This is, firstly, because GPs do not receive payment for registering as a permanent patient anyone of no fixed residence; they can claim payment if they register such patients as temporary residents, but they are reluctant to do this. Secondly, such patients often turn up at surgeries in a disorderly state and are, consequently, an unwelcome 'problem'. In theory, every UK citizen has the right to register with a GP, but in practice GPs and their receptionists can refuse entry to patients of no fixed abode.

In 1980 I took up the post of 'experienced nurse to run the Primary Medical Care Project in a day centre for vagrant alcoholics'. I recognised that a traditional nursing role, with no formal diagnostic skills or autonomy of action, would not meet the health needs of these patients, nor would it be effective primary health care. In addition to nursing care, destitute people with many problems require rigorous skills in history taking, examination, diagnosis, treatment or referral, and preventive measures plus a huge amount of cajoling, persuading and counselling. It was clear to me that anything less would be irresponsible and, indeed, dangerous, given the magnitude of the presenting problems.

Local GPs, however, were not pleased by my efforts to respond to these patients. They were unhelpful when I tried to refer patients to them, and the patients themselves often refused a second consultation with them, fearing an ungracious reception. The GPs usually refused my request to refer a homeless patient to a specialist (Burke-Masters, 1986). I was, therefore, led to take my controversial clinical initiative and become an autonomous nurse practitioner following the American model in order to meet pressing needs based on my extended knowledge and skills learnt in the Third World.

The nature of the solution

A local GP, Dr Maurice Rosen, supplied me with small bulk stocks of mutually agreed prescription-only medicines and preparations, lotions and dressings. As accurate diagnosis depends on careful history taking and examination, I acquired the necessary tools (e.g. stethoscope, otoscope), and developed my existing skills to look, listen and feel with reasonable accomplishment. I gradually established links with hospital consultants who accepted my referrals and corresponded with me fully. There developed a heartening mutual esteem.

Acquiring the skills to practise good primary health care is a life-long effort, and to this end some of the consultants allowed me into their clinics and ward rounds, and I read journals regularly. I also undertook, as an evening student, a BSc honours degree in psychology. Through this I have gained some insight into personality: motivation, perception, learning, intelligence, the neuroses and psychoses. How have I put my learning experiences into practice?

Table 7.3   Medicines and instruments used by Sister Burke-Masters

Prescribable medicines and preparations	Other medications and preparations
Tabs. ampicillin 250 mg	Mist. Benylin & davenol
Tabs. penicillin 250 mg	Mist. asilone
Tabs. Septrin	Mist. mag. trisilicate
Tabs. ibuprofen 400 mg	Tabs. asilone
Tabs. phenytoin 50 mg	Tabs. paracetamol
Tabs. salbutamol 4 mg	Tabs. vit. B complex
Salbutamol inhaler	Tabs. vit. B1 (thiamine)
Tabs. chlorpromazine 25 mg	Loz. Strepsils
Tabs. promethazine 10 mg & 25 mg	Cerumol gutt.
Diazepam 10 mg. I.M.I × 2 amps	Paste mag. sulphate
Tabs. diazepam 10 mg	Calamine lotion
Tabs. codeine phosphate 30 mg	Caladryl lotion
Tabs. cimetidine 400 mg	Aserbine ung.
Tabs. Orovite	Shampoo dicophane 1% & lindane 1%
Tabs. carbamazepine 200 mg	Aqueous cream
Sachets amoxycillin 3 g	Karvol caps.
Tabs. tetracycline 250 mg	Tinct. benzoin
Tabs. erythromycin 250 mg	Tinct. gentian violet
Tabs. frumil	Paraffin gauze
Tabs. digoxin 0.125 mg	Sofra tulle
Chloramphenicol gutt. for ears 10%	Savlon sachets
Chloramphenicol ung. for eyes 1%	Normal saline for eyes
Fusidic acid ung.	Chlorhexidine in spirit
Tetracycline ung.	Disidane spray
Betamethazone ung. & hydrocortisone 1%	Tineafax powder
Coal tar & salicylic acid ung.	Eusol
Ephedrine nasal gutt.	Albustix
Clotrimazole ung. 1%	Clinistix
Oilatum ung.	Melolin
Tabs. Pentazocine 25 mg	A range of sterile and non-sterile
Zinc paste bandages	dressings
Cream dithranol 0.25%	
Sod. bic. gutt. for ears	

Instruments

Stethoscope	Brook airway
Otoscope	Rubber airways
Neurological hammer	Disposable gloves
Sphygmomanometer	Disposable tongue depressors
Ear syringing equipment	Thermometer
Peak flow meter	Ophthalmoscope
Suture scissors	Fetal stethoscope
Forceps	

Modus operandi

Every patient's presenting problem is carefully investigated and I have developed the following structure:

- Take a careful history
- Perform an appropriate examination
- Form an impression with alternative strategies

Depending on the outcome of these, I usually take up one or more of the following options:

1 Offer explanation, reassurance, advice and answer questions;
2 Treat with available medication, e.g. antibiotics (see Table 7.3 for my limited list);
3 Refer to a consultant, or elsewhere as appropriate. This involves a careful letter containing the medical history, clinical findings, my tentative impressions and any treatment given. Then I have to do endless reminding and cajoling of patients to attend the appointment: about 90% of referrals are successful. I also arrange the appointment.

A card index system of patients' details is kept, which records name, date of birth, address, if any, and dates of consultations. Cross-referenced clinical data are kept separately.

I try to put the patient's organic complaint into a social and emotional perspective in my clinical assessment and support. I keep the consultation formal, as this gently discourages any signs of familiarity. I admit to needing a little space, even if patients do not.

The range of complaints I deal with is wide: from cut fingers to Huntington's chorea; from sore feet to cancer; from simple headaches to fractured skulls; from minor neuroses to schizophrenia; chest infections including tuberculosis; epilepsy, peptic ulcers, venous ulcers, arthritis and many more. The vast majority are common ailments, including upper respiratory tract infections, diarrhoea, ear, eye and skin infections, abdominal problems, insomnia, burns, lacerations, haemorrhoids and many non-specific aches and pains. Many patients also feel anxious, lonely and miserable and their pasts include unfulfilled hopes and desires, personal tragedies and experience of social inadequacy. These have often led to aggression, despair, numerous psychological problems, and drug and alcohol abuse.

One of my main tools is listening but I feel that one of my most useful skills is to try to help patients to face up to themselves and their problems – which sometimes means broaching the delicate issue of bad behaviour. This is carried out in a climate of mutual respect and the patients are amazingly receptive to it.

Some descriptive statistics

Annual analysis of practice records shows:

- Approximately 2700 annual consultations
- 12–15 daily consultations, on average (range 5–21)
- Approximately 340 referrals
- 2000 people on my list at April 1987
- Most patients, 98%, are male
- Age range of patients seen is 16–80 years
- 2% or less were registered with a GP and these had an address (none of those with no fixed address were registered with a GP)

In 1987, my seventh year of practice, I made 498 referrals to other professionals. The hospital consultant referrals followed the normal out-patients pattern.

Responsibility and support

Being clinically autonomous (able to act independently on the basis of my own diagnoses), I take personal responsibility for all my actions. The major areas are as follows:

1   The vast majority of decisions concerning diagnosis and treatment are my sole responsibility. When uncertain, a second opinion is always sought either from a hospital doctor or my supporting GP (Maurice Rosen).
2   Administering, recording, storing and checking of all medications. Prescribable druges are detailed in independent records, and all tablets are accounted for. Expiry dates are checked, all medications are stored correctly. Patients are well counselled about how to take them (Rosen, 1986).
3   I keep detailed and properly organised notes and records.
4   I update and develop my knowledge.

My GP colleague provides support, and visits me fortnightly to discuss any problems, supply medication, and check the notes, referral letters and replies.

Persona non grata

Despite the undeniable success of my innovation (Hadridge, 1987), I was, and still am, ignored by the medical and nursing establishment. The attitude of the Department of Health and Social Security is that doctors must provide a service for the homeless, although this service is inadequate. Some voluntary bodies like Shelter, No Fixed Abode and the Campaign for the Homeless and Rootless, while admitting that existing services are appalling, call my work a 'second-class service' but some consultants judge it to be a first-rate service (Wheeler, in Sharron, 1984). Some GPs have called me a 'pseudo-service' (McCormack & Donovan, 1983), and I have defended my integrity (Burke-Masters, 1983). The Royal College of Nursing (RCN) rejected my first application for indemnity in 1983, saying I had over-stepped my brief (Rye, 1983, personal correspondence). The Medical Defence Union did likewise but admitted that I was practising safe medicine and was almost certainly a low risk. The biggest blow came from the least expected quarter: St. George's Men's Care Unit, where I had been employed for four and a half years to run the surgery. The Unit issued a statement that either I obtain establishment recognition for my work or I must stop treating patients. Suppression was complete when the Pharmaceutical Society, having read an article about my work in *The Guardian* (Sharron, 1984), asked the St George's Men's Care parson to remove my prescription-only medication to a local chemist, which he did. I was then threatened with two years in prison, but following publicity in the press and on television, they withdrew their complaints. Throughout all this few nurses came to my aid, some condemned my work (e.g. Lock, 1985). I replied in the *Nursing Times*, defending my work (Burke-Masters, 1985). For a year I did not work.

In March, 1986, I completed the negotiations for the reestablishment of the practice under the auspices of the Manna Centre – a day centre for homeless and destitute men in the London Bridge area. The RCN has now granted indemnity insurance for all aspects of my work, and they have assured me that they will take to the High Court anyone who attempts to sabotage my practice again. The Manna Society and Dr Rosen have been instrumental in obtaining a three-year grant for me from the King's Fund. Various drug companies now generously donate the medicines I use. I can request radiographs (by arrangement with Guy's Hospital), and the Family Practitioner Committee accepts my applications for medical cards for my patients.

Discussion

After seven years as a clinically autonomous nurse practitioner, I feel that special groups with special needs require a special service. My patients cannot be properly provided for in a conventional general practice.

I am clearly a substitute doctor – a nurse with an extended role into medicine. I was forced to break the rules because the rules excluded my patients from proper care. I am not interested in constructing models of nursing, but I am passionately interested in meeting health needs. What is wrong with a nurse carrying out a medical procedure (e.g. giving penicillin) if she/he has the expertise? While the spin-off from my work has been more power and autonomy, this was not my primary motive.

While my work is lawful, it is still unsanctioned by the state. It does not require a change in law to grant recognition to my work. The Medicines (Prescription only) Amendment (no. 2) Order, 1978, could be applied to me. This amendment was made for occupational health nurses. Under it, a contract is agreed by both the doctor and nurse on the supply and administration of prescription only medicines, taking knowledge and competence into account (Cowper, 1986). This is how my supervisory GP and I function with regard to medicines. We discuss, agree, I carry out the practice, and he supports me. General practitioners are not always the best qualified people to provide all primary care. To all nurses who feel able and who have the opportunity, I say: 'Do not go where the path may lead; go instead where there is no path and leave a trail'.

References

Allen M, Frasure-Smith N & Gottlieb L (1982) What makes a 'good' nurse? *Canadian Nurse*, **78**, 42–5

Argyle M (1983) *The Psychology of Interpersonal Behaviour*. Harmondsworth, Penguin Books

Burke-Masters B (1983) Pseudo tags won't stick. *Doctor*, October 13, 53

Burke-Masters B (1985) Medicine for the poor. *Nursing Times*, June 5, 14–15

Burke-Masters B (1986) The autonomous nurse practitioner: an answer to a chronic problem of primary care. *The Lancet*, **i**, 1266

Cartwright A (1967) *Patients and their Doctors*. London: Routledge and Kegan Paul

Cartwright A & Anderson R (1981) *General Practice Revisited*. London: Tavistock Press

Cowper B (1986) Prescribing by nurse practitioners *Lancet*, **ii**, 1266

Department of Health and Social Security (1980) *Report of the Working Party on Inequalities in Health (Black Report)*. London: DHSS

Griffiths R (1981) *Introduction to the Report of the Conference Arranged by the Association of Community Health Councils for England and Wales: The Campaign for the Homeless and Rootless*. London: ACHEW

Hadridge P (1987) The plight of homeless families. *Congress Issue of the Nursing Standard*, **3**, 8

Hoole A J, Greenberg R A & Pickard C G (1982) *Patient Care Guidlines for Nurse Practioners*. Boston: Little Brown

Lock K (1985) The danger of clinics especially for the homeless. *Nursing Times*, May 8, 19

McCormack M & Donovan M (1983) GPs split over vagrant problem. *Doctor*, September 8, 2

Mackichan N D, (1976) *The General Practitioner and the Primary Health Care Team*. London: Pitman

Morrell D C, Evans M E, Morris R W & Roland M D (1986) The five-minute consultation: effect of time constraint on verbal communication. *British Medical Journal*, **292**, 874–876

Peplau H E (1952) *Interpersonal Relations in Nursing*. New York: Pitman

Rosen M (1986) Prescribing by nurse practitioners. *The Lancet*, **ii**(8498), 107

Sharron H (1984) The (rather embarrassing) sister of mercy. *The Guardian*, December 19, 7

Stilwell B (1985) Prevention and health: the concern of nursing. *Journal of the Royal Society of Health*, **105**, 60–62

8

The Extended Role of Practice Nurses in Preventive Health Care

GODFREY FOWLER   ELAINE FULLARD   J A MUIR GRAY

Introduction

'About a half of all strokes and a quarter of deaths from coronary heart disease in people under 70 are probably preventable by the application of existing knowledge.'

This was the conclusion of the Royal College of General Practitioners (1981) report on prevention of arterial disease in general practice. It is the contribution that practice nurses have made towards closing this gap between *knowledge* and *action* that will be demonstrated in this chapter.

So much progress and success in reducing morbidity and mortality has been achieved by midwives, doctors and health visitors in antenatal and child care. This good example of a systematic and team approach needs to be translated to other age groups to improve other aspects of health care.

Research shows that, besides the preventability of heart attack and strokes, the following burden is preventable:

- 30% of cancers (including half of cervical cancer and a third of breast cancer)
- 70% of bronchitis and emphysema
- 95% of amputations

This chapter will, therefore, focus primarily on the practice nurse's role in screening for cardiovascular risk factors and offering help and advice in managing risk factors. The opportunity exists, however, to extend the work to cervical cytology screening and immunisation.

The potential of the primary health care team

The conventional role of medical care is the management of illness and disease. Doctors and nurses are trained to detect, diagnose, manage and, wherever possible, cure disease. Disease prevention and health promotion require a rather different philosophical approach and are accorded low priority. This may seem strange, given that the Latin origin of the word 'doctor' is 'teacher'. but being a teacher is more mundane and less exciting than being a magician with a therapeutic wand.

The adequacy of what one might call a 'symptom-swatting' approach in primary care is being increasingly questioned. The role of what Julian Tudor Hart described as a 'medical shop keeper in a corner shop' is too narrow (Hart, 1981). However, the practice nurse, by being a member of the primary health care team, is in a unique situation to provide health promotion and anticipatory care.

Primary care has so many advantages because:

1 *Access to the public*
   ● In the UK at least 98% of the population are registered with a general practitioner.
   ● 75% of the practice population will consult their general practitioner or nurse within a year and at least 90% within five years, providing a 'ready-made' opportunity for offering a screening programme.
2 *Access to the high risk groups*
   ● Smokers consult twice as often as non-smokers.
   ● People in the lower social classes (IIIM, IV and V), in whom coronary heart disease and cancers are more common, consult more frequently than professional people (Office of Population Censuses and Surveys, 1980).
   ● The needs of the unemployed and self-employed people, who would miss out on offers of screening in the workplace, can be met. Unemployed people have been found to suffer more illness than those in employment.
3 *The potency of the health professionals*
   ● General practitioners and nurses have high credibility with the public; for example, 95% of the public tend to trust their family doctor, and 87% their local nurse or health visitor as a reliable source of health information (Health Education Authority/Consumers Association, 1982).
   ● Of all the practice services available, patients thought that the presence of a practice nurse was the most important asset (Consumers Association, 1987).
   ● General practitioners (Russell *et al*, 1979) and nurses (Kenkre *et al*, 1985) have proved to be effective in helping people to give up smoking.
   ● The team, all being in the same building, have the benefit of the opportunity for easy, quick and efficient patient referral; for example,

very powerful in health education

should a nurse wish to ask her colleague general practitioner to recheck a blood pressure, this can easily be done.
- Patients consulting *expect* advice on health promotion (Wallace & Haines, 1984).
- Communication is one-to-one and can therefore be individual to meet personal needs.

The potential–achievement gap

However, there is a big gap between this potential and its achievement. Many opportunities for preventive medicine and health promotion go begging and general practice records contain little information about, for example, smoking and drinking habits, dietary habits, weight, exercise or even blood pressure management.

Undoubtedly, some of the responsibility for this failure lies with nursing education. Most basic medical and nursing education remains almost entirely hospital-based with emphasis on advanced disease and acute, even heroic, medical care. 'Salvage' is rated highly; prevention is at the bottom of the pile.

A major constraint in general practice is also the brevity of consultations. One answer might be a reduction in list sizes; another is to use the potential of the primary health care team. At present, only 15% of practices in the UK are up to their reimbursable limit of two ancillary staff per GP. In Oxfordshire (population: 530 000), for example, there is a potential for the immediate employment of 168 extra half-time practice nurses. Any practice teams employing these nurses would be eligible to reclaim 70% of their salary costs as part of the Family Practitioner Committee reimbursement scheme. A nurse working for ten hours per week would result in a net cost to the practice of less than £10. For a typical group practice of about 10 000 patients, this number of hours has proved sufficient for the nurse to screen the population in the research study detailed below.

The Oxford Prevention of Heart Attack and Stroke Project

In 1982 we initiated a research project to explore the role of practice nurses in prevention and the employment of a nurse called a 'facilitator' (Fullard) to stimulate, initiate, educate and maintain such activity in a number of practices.

The project arose from our belief that what primary care teams need is not more exhortation but information, advice and practical help to make use of their opportunities and potential. It was initially concerned with testing the feasibility of the 1981 Royal College of General Practitioner's Report *Prevention of Arterial Disease in General Practice*, with the aim of ensuring that, starting with the 35–64 age group, all patients had at least one recording of blood pressure every five years, were asked and advised about smoking, and were weighed and given dietary advice.

The design of the project was a controlled trial with intervention and control practices. The *facilitator* introduced the screening package to the practices, providing appropriate training for the practice staff (particularly receptionists and practice nurses) and offered continuing advice and support (Fullard *et al*, 1987). A *prevention nurse* was either specially employed by the practice for the job or was an existing nurse in the practice who extended the number of hours that she worked.

The method of screening

Patients in the target age group who were attending the practice for any reason were invited by the receptionist to see the nurse for a brief health check (subsequently nicknamed 'a human MOT'). This avoided both the time and cost of sending postal invitations. Some nurses offered clinics in the mornings and evenings to meet the needs of the working population.

Health checks took about 20 minutes and were either organised in special sessions by the nurse in health-check clinics or interspersed with her other treatment room work. The nurse asked about relevant family history and diabetes, recorded blood pressure, measured weight and height, enquired about diet, alcohol and (where appropriate) oral contraception, and recorded smoking habits. Blood pressure measurement and the subsequent course of action followed a protocol (Fig. 8.1) and smoking and dietary advice was given in accordance with guidelines.

Blood lipids were measured selectively only in those with a personal or family history of coronary heart disease at or below the age of 55 and in patients with multiple risk factors. Tests for blood sugar were only carried out for those who were seriously obese (more than 30% overweight) or who had a family history of diabetes.

Information was recorded in the notes on a special health summary card (Fig. 8.2) and the outside of the patient's records labelled with the date for next review.

Evaluation was by record audit which measured changes in the recording of risk factors in patients' notes. The records of patients in the target age groups were searched for any recording of blood pressure, weight or any mention of smoking habit within the previous five years. The initial audit covered the five year period up to 1 April 1982 (the date of first contact with the intervention practices) and the second audit covered the five year period ending 30 September 1984 (i.e. two and a half years after the intervention was started). Control practices were not recruited until the intervention was completed (to avoid the influence of such recruitment on behaviour) and data collection in the control practices was therefore necessarily retrospective.

The outcome measurement was the recording of risk factors in patients' records, this being a measure of professional behaviour in practices. It was recognised that this was only the initial step in risk factor ascertainment and management, and that changes in risk factors and, of course, morbidity and mortality are more significant.

The research team relied on the strong epidemiological evidence from large trials with longer intervention and follow-up times. These have shown that controlling hypertension, for example, does reduce the incidence of strokes (Hypertension Detection and Follow-up Co-operative Group, 1979; Helgeland,

1980; Australian National Blood Pressure Study Management Committee, 1980). Finland provides another good example of action being taken with a resultant decrease of 25% in the heart disease rate within 15 years (Puska *et al*, 1983).

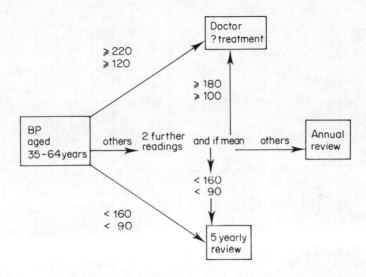

NB 1   Patient sitting

2   Note fear/anxiety/anger/cold, if present

3   ? Empty bladder

4   ? Adequate cuff to encircle arm

5   Rate of fall of pressure 2 mmHg/s

6   Record to nearest 2 mmHg

7   DBP Phase V((complete absence of sound unless this is zero, then use Phase IV (muffling) and record 'IV' after recording in medical notes

Fig. 8.1   Nurse blood pressure protocol

The initial audit demonstrated low levels of recording of the three risk factors in all practices, with only small differences between the practices, whether in intervention or in control. Initially, blood pressure was recorded in 35% of the medical notes in intervention practices (compared with 37% in controls), smoking habit in 11% in intervention practices (12% in controls), and weight or an indication of obesity in 12% of intervention practices (13% in controls). These differences between intervention and control practices were not significant, indicating that they were well matched. However, the final audit showed that although there were substantial increases in the recording of blood pressure, smoking habit and weight in all practices, this was much greater in the intervention practices than it was in the controls.

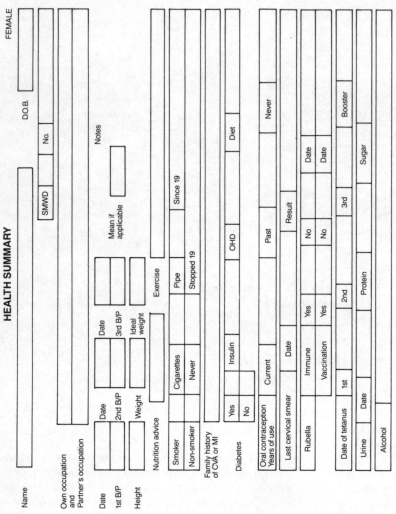

HEALTH SUMMARY

Name _____ **D.O.B.** _____ **FEMALE**

Own occupation
and _____ **SMWD** __ **No.** __
Partner's occupation

	Date	2nd B/P	Date	3rd B/P	
1st B/P					**Mean if applicable**

Notes
_____

Height | **Weight** | **Ideal weight** |

Nutrition advice _____ **Exercise** _____

| **Smoker** | Cigarettes | Pipe | Since 19 |
| **Non-smoker** | Never | Stopped 19 |

Family history of CVA or MI _____

| **Diabetes** | Yes | Insulin | OHD | Diet |
| | No | | | |

Oral contraception
Years of use | Current | Past | Never |

Last cervical smear | Date | Result |

| **Rubella** | Immune | Yes | No | Date |
| **Vaccination** | Yes | No | Date |

| **Date of tetanus** | 1st | 2nd | 3rd | Booster |

Urine | Date | Protein | Sugar |

Alcohol _____

Notes / Advice given / Further action

CONTINUATION

Date	B/P	Smoking	Weight	Contraceptive change	Rubella	Tetanus	Cervical smear		

Printed as a service to the Medical Profession by
Stuart Pharmaceuticals Limited

Fig. 8.2   Health summary record sheet (female)

After the two and a half year interval, 59% of records in intervention practices had a blood pressure recording (49% in controls), 49% a mention of smoking habit (21% in controls) and 45% a measurement of weight (19% in controls). Numerically, 1022 extra people had their blood pressure recorded, 2327 their smoking habits recorded and 2158 their weight in the three intervention practices, compared with the controls (Fig. 3). Eighty-four patients with sustained blood pressure readings at or above 180/100 were identified, including three patients with sustained measurements greater than 220/120.

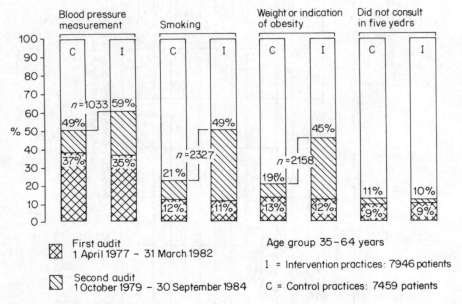

Fig. 8.3   Audit of improvements in recording blood pressure movements, smoking habits and weight (or an indication of obesity). The differences between control and intervention practices are highly significant ($p < 0.001$) for all three items. (Fullard *et al*, 1987: reproduced with the permission of the editor of the *British Medical Journal*)

Thus, the introduction into intervention practices of a systematic case-finding approach, using practice nurses to conduct health checks, and with the help of a facilitator as an informal adviser/resource agent and trainer, substantially enhances ascertainment of risk factors.The increase in blood pressure recordings was doubled, the increase in recording smoking habits quadrupled and weight recording increased more than five fold in the intervention practices compared with the controls (Fullard *et al*, 1987).

General practitioners incurred some extra costs by extending the number of practice nurse hours but these, as indicated earlier, were modest. Equally, extra work for doctors is generated by detection of hypertensive patients needing treatment but few would deny the value of this. The nurses are responsible for recalling the borderline hypertensives. These patients accounted for 76% of the newly diagnosed hypertension. For practice nurses this new, extended role is challenging and satisfying. They become full professional partners in the primary care team. Although health visitors can, of course, do the job, in many situations they are too busy to take on this additional work.

Receptionists have found their role enhanced by their participation in the preventive programme. They have enjoyed initiating the offer of appointments instead of merely responding to patients' requests for them.

More importantly, the patients have responded enthusiastically with only 3% of the first 4 000 declining the offer of a health check. Results of a questionnaire survey on patients' attitudes to health checks indicate that the majority of patients were reassured and wanted even more information (Anderson, 1986, personal communication). More than half the practices in Oxfordshire have now adopted the same or similar screening programmes. In collaboration with the Chest, Heart and Stroke Association (who originally funded the research) and the Health Education Authority, the Oxfordshire Health Authority has now established a Centre for Prevention in Primary Care which acts as a resource centre. A national development programmme is in hand and 38 other health authorities have now appointed facilitators on the same or a similar model. There are such appointments in England, Wales, Scotland and Northern Ireland.

The role of the facilitator

A facilitator is someone with a primary health care background, who literally makes things easy or easier. He or she is employed by the district health authority or family practitioner committee to offer help to interested practices in extending their role in preventive medicine.

Facilitators act as cross-pollinators of good ideas to other practices that may be thinking about starting a systematic approach to screening. The role includes:

1   Meeting the practice manager and receptionists and, if needed, helping them to invite in the first few patients. The general practitioner has an important role in encouraging and validating the invitation. the facilitator may suggest that every member of the team has an MOT themselves before the screening begins. The same principle is involved as in selling washing powder − it probably sells much better if you use it yourself!
2   Providing a back-up service. For example, a facilitator has examples of health education literature, a supply of coloured height/weight charts as teaching aids for weight reduction and examples of recall letters for mild hypertensives.

The emphasis is on practical help, but, to enable the facilitator to act as a temporary guest and informal adviser to the next practice interested, she does not carry out the clinical work herself. However, since most of the facilitators are nurses, should a screening nurse be suddenly off sick, the facilitator can, with the practice's permission, help out by conducting a clinic.

Summary of the project

The study has demonstrated that risk factor ascertainment in primary care can be substantially improved by an opportunistic, systematic approach involving practice nurses. It shows a good example of how development of the role of practice nurses can bring about major changes in primary care. A facilitator, too, can initiate and maintain a programme in a number of practices more quickly and effectively than would occur without such support, and this model can undoubtedly be applied to other aspects of prevention and general practice care.

Practical implications for practice nurses

Training needs

Developing new roles means that new skills in listening and counselling the patients are required. The nurses screening for cardiovascular risk factors have gained some of the skills by attending courses provided either by the local health education unit or by enrolling for the Certificate in Health Education offered by many colleges of further education. Study days on hypertension for nurses in general practice are held in Birmingham and there are now several practice nurse courses, some of which have been approved by the English National Board (ENB). District facilitators have information on ENB courses and other study days provided by health authorities, family practitioner committees or facilitators in other districts.

Deciding on a policy for blood pressure referral is a good opportunity for a team to discuss criteria of measurement. Accurate and consistent measurement of blood pressure is difficult to achieve because of variations in recording the final sounds. The World Health Organization recommends that diastolic V (complete absence of sound) is used since there are fewer discrepancies in this measurement than diastolic IV (muffling). However, if muffling is decided upon, Phase IV (the diastolic reading) needs to be noted in the records for other members of the team to take account of differences in recordings. Each member of the team needs to be supplied with an outsize blood pressure cuff to ensure accuracy of measurement in obese patients. Four-headed training stethoscopes may be purchased. A team can therefore listen to one blood pressure to see if the members all obtain the same reading. Excellent videotapes have been produced on the measurement of blood pressure, which can be used in the same way.

Starting a screening programme is an ideal time to ensure that all the sphygmomanometers have been checked within the last six months. Several of the pharmaceutical companies offer this service should it not be possible to take the instrument to the medical equipment supplier. It is also well worth while to check the weighing scales for accuracy.

Information about local slimming, exercise and relaxation classes, smoking cessation groups and other health resources provided by the community is invaluable. Many patients who are identified with, for example, obesity, may be offered group support in addition to individual counselling by the nurse in the practice.

Keeping the screening programmes going – some recipes for success

One of the project advisers (Gray, 1987, personal communication) has proposed that the following interventions will help progress with the development of new roles:

Interventions likely to help professionals to improve their performance
1   Focusing on people;
2   Education in the workplace;
3   Knocking down the barriers to better performance;
4   Practical assistance with steps to improve performance, for example by passing on tips from others, by help with the work required to audit or change ways of working;
5   Opportunities for teams to learn together;
6   Quantitative feedback about performance;
7   Opportunity to compare performance with that of others;
8   Giving positive feedback first;
9   Enthusiasm;
10   Interventions that persist over a period of time;
11   Interventions that include more than one education approach;
12   One-to-one teaching for the transmission of skills.

Interventions likely to be unhelpful in improving performance
1   Focusing on organisations;
2   Centralised education;
3   Teaching that ignores barriers such as lack of time or resources;
4   Vague exhortations and advice such as 'do better';
5   All learning done in individual professional groups;
6   Vague unquantifiable feedback;
7   Interventions given to a professional or team in isolation;
8   Negative feedback given first;
9   Unenthusiastic interventions;
10   Transient interventions;
11   Interventions that have only one approach;
12   Group teaching for skill transmission.

Putting Gray's recommendations into action has been one of the keys to enthusiastic response by the practice teams.

Personal contact has been found to be a strong factor in overcoming barriers to change (Horder *et al*, 1986), and much of the facilitator's work described earlier is practice based. He or she can help practices to establish ways for teams to monitor their own successes or failures in their screening programmes.

Evaluating practice progress

The World Health Organization has set its goal of 'Health for All by the Year 2000'. Practice teams can likewise set a target of offering, for example, a health check to everyone within a five year period. Charts similar to those produced for raising money to 'repair the church roof' are a way of indicating progress and help to motivate and inform everyone of steps towards achieving the agreed goal.

An audit, that is, a review of the medical records, is a way of assessing the percentage of adults who have already been screened, for example, for hypertension. Audit, in itself, has an impact on professional behaviour (Fleming & Lawrence, 1983). Facilitators can offer help in selecting a 10% sample and supplying audit guidelines. Some practices employ temporary help for this audit, often a nurse or a receptionist. It should not be a mammoth task: for instance, it took a practice with 9 000 patients only 26 hours to do a 1 in 10 sample audit of their middle-aged adults. This provided them with a baseline before starting a full programme and cost less than £20 (after allowing for the family practitioner committee staff salaries reimbursement scheme and tax relief).

The district facilitator may be able to offer a *Rent-an-Audit* team. The Oxfordshire team consists of two trained auditors who work to a protocol with strict confidentiality for the patients and the practice. These professionals may be hired by a practice for a small charge and can usually conduct an audit in two or three afternoons with minimal disturbance to the practice.

Evaluation of the numbers of patients seen and risk factors that have been identified can be made by keeping a *log book* that involves little clerical work. The log book can give an indication to the team of the gender and age group of patients attending the health checks, the number who do not arrive, women with overdue smear tests and referral rates for tetanus boosters, hypertension and cholesterol tests. In addition, the log books give a good excuse for the team to celebrate when, for example, the hundredth patient has been screened.

Presentation of *case studies* at practice meetings maintains enthusiasm and interest in the programme. Evaluation of *recall* for newly diagnosed hypertensives by maintaining a card index register in a box file or by registering recalls on a computer are ways of ensuring that risk factors are followed up.

Finally, and most important of all, *the patients' needs*, expectations and experience of the screening programme can be measured. An anonymous questionnaire could be returned by a sample of patients. This would need to include those accepting and declining the invitation. Informal verbal feedback is useful and a little positive feedback from patients encourages the team enormously. A survey of patients in Oxford by Robert Anderson found that preventive medicine is welcomed by patients so any practice embarking on a screening programme should find it a rewarding and enjoyable experience (Anderson, 1987).

A team can derive great job satisfaction, too, from the feeling that by screening their population they are 'on top of the problem', rather than the frustration of the 'symptom swatting' approach described earlier. By offering anticipatory care a team can justly feel that they are making a contribution to reducing much of the misery and disability of premature strokes and the pain for the bereaved of victims of early heart attacks.

Protected time is needed, since the demands on the team for traditional care are great. By employing a nurse solely for health checks or a cervical cytology clinic ensures that prevention is not 'pushed out'.

Conclusion

Perhaps one of the most exciting developments of the practice nurse is the increasing interest in health rather than illness. Health has often been regarded as rather boring in comparison with the discovery of someone with very high blood pressure. As one nurse stated: It is so nice to see so many people who are well. With so much potential for the employment of practice nurses and the enthusiasm and commitment with which nurses are extending their role, it may be the nurse who will lead the team in the health promotion of the future.

References

Anderson R (1987) Effectiveness of practice nurses in preventive care from the patient's point of view. Paper presented at *The Nurse Practitioner and the Practice Nurse. Which way Next?* Conference held at St Bartholomew's Hospital, London, January 1987

Australian National Blood Pressure Study Management Committee (1980) The Australian therapeutic trial in mild hypertension. *Lancet*, **i**, 1261–1267

Consumers Association (1987) *'Which' Survey of Practice Services*. London: Consumers Association

Fleming D M & Lawrence M S T A (1983) Impact of audit on preventive measures. *British Medical Journal*, **287**, 1582–1584

Fullard E M, Fowler G H & Gray J A M (1987) Promoting prevention in primary care: a controlled trial of low-technology, low cost approach. *British Medical Journal*, **294**, 1080–1082

Hart J T (1981) A new kind of doctor. *Journal of the Royal Society of Medicine*, **74**, 871–883

Health Education Authority/Consumers Association (1982) *General Health Survey – Reliability of Health Advice*. London: Health Education Authority

Helgeland D (1980) Treatment of mild hypertension: a five year controlled drug trial. The Oslo study. *American Journal of Medicine*, **60**, 725–732

Horder J, Bosanquet N & Stocking B (1986) Ways of influencing the behaviour of general practitioners. *Journal of the Royal College of General Practitioners*, **36**, 517–521

Hypertension Detection and Follow-up Co-operative Group (1979) Five year findings of the hypertension detection and follow-up programme: reduction in mortality of persons with high blood pressure, including mild hypertension. *Journal of the American Medical Association*, **242**, 2562–2571

Kenkre J, Drury V W M & Lancashire R J (1985) Nurse management of hypertension clinics in general practice assisted by a computer. *Family Practice*, **2**, 17–22

Office of Population Censuses and Surveys (1980) *General Household Survey 1978*, Series GHS No. 8. London: HMSO

Puska P, Nissinen A, Salonen J T et al (1983) Ten years of the North Karelia project: results with community based prevention of coronary heart disease. *Scandanavian Journal of Social Medicine*, **11**, 65–68

Royal College of General Practitioners (1981) *Prevention of Arterial Disease in General Practice*. Report from general practice No. 20. London: Royal College of General Practitioners

Russell M A H, Wilson C, Taylor C & Baker C D (1979) Effect of general practitioners' advice against smoking. *British Medical Journal*, **2**, 231–235

Wallace P G & Haines A P (1984) General practitioners and health promotion: what patients think. *British Medical Journal*, **289**, 534–536

9
Survey of Practice Nurses in the UK – Their Extended Roles

LYNNE CATER   PAMELA HAWTHORN

Introduction

In 1961 it was still comparatively rare for nurses in Britain to work directly with general practitioners, and there was little information about their work (Cartwright & Scott, 1961). Reedy (1972a) did not find that any large scale surveys of practice nurse employment had been completed. Ten years later, Bowling (1981a), after reviewing the literature, suggested that little was known about the extent and type of delegation of work to nurses in British general practice but later concluded:

> 'the more complex the task, the less likely the nurse is, especially in the case of attached nurses, to perform it.'   (Bowling, 1981b)

Early studies showed that the nurse's role in the surgery was mainly limited to carrying out tasks that were traditionally regarded as 'nursing' (Cartwright & Scott, 1961; Murray, 1967; Baldwin, 1967; Marsh, 1967). Marsh (1976, 1978) discussed how the role of nurses working in the surgery was altering to include women's health screening and family planning, initiating investigations according to protocols, managing minor illnesses, and following up patients with chronic diseases. Men's health clinics were also conducted by nurses (Marsh & Chew, 1984). Reedy (1972b) identified the tasks that had been carried out by nurses working in the surgery, and reported in the literature, over the preceding

20 years. He found that many of the tasks were common nursing tasks, whilst some would ordinarily have been performed by other 'professions supplementary to medicine'. In several areas he thought that the privately employed practice nurse's territory appeared to overlap with that of the health visitor. Marsh (1985), in a forward-looking article, outlined areas of current nursing work which either attached district nurses and health visitors or privately employed practice nurses might do.

A scheme that was started in Oxfordshire has been extensively copied (Fullard *et al*, 1984). There, a facilitator encourages practices to instigate preventive medicine by employing practice nurses to identify, and attempt to modify, risk factors associated with heart disease and stroke (see Chapter 8).

Although the role of the practice nurse employed by the general practitioner appears to be well documented, much of the literature relating to practice nurses is anecdotal (Murray, 1967; Marsh, 1967; Mottram, 1968; Pearson, 1985; Hudson, 1985). Research has been mostly confined to studies with limited samples of either nurses or practices, and was mainly concerned with descriptions of the nurses' work (Cartwright & Scott, 1961; Hodgkin & Gillie, 1968; Weston Smith & O'Donovan, 1970; Bain & Haines, 1974; Walters *et al*, 1980; Marriott, 1981). Other writers have extolled the usefulness of the practice nurse (Powell, 1984; Hart, 1985; Laurance, 1985).

The work of nurses employed by the local health authority, in the treatment rooms of health centres and surgeries, has also been described (Dixon, 1969; Hockey, 1972; Nimmo, 1978a, 1978b; McIntosh, 1979; Goddard, 1981; Dopson, 1984). It has been compared with that of nurses employed by general practitioners (Reedy *et al*, 1980a; 1980b; Bowling, 1981a; Dunnell & Dobbs, 1980). More recently, health authority nurses and health visitors have been reported as running men's health clinics (Carroll-Williams & Allen, 1984; Pownall, 1985; Deans & Hoskins, 1987), and assisting the general practitioner with caring for patients with chronic diseases (Smith and Bignell, 1987).

A review of the literature indicates an evolution of privately employed practice nurses' work patterns over time, particularly in the last decade. Their role as listener, adviser and agent of first contact has continued to develop, and technical procedures and, more recently, screening or health promotion have been added to their traditional treatment work.

In the report from the Royal College of Nursing (1984), it was noted that there is a wide variation in the extent and nature of these nurses' contribution to the practice workload. Some nurses include receptionists' duties as part of their work (Cornwall and Isles of Scilly Family Practitioner Committee, 1986), others adopt a more autonomous nurse practitioner role (Allen, 1976; Stilwell, 1984; Vousden, 1985; Diamond, 1986; Doyle, 1987).

Hall (1982) interviewed Stilwell and described her as 'the first nurse practitioner in Britain'. They agreed that the differences between her work as a nurse practitioner and that of experienced and well directed practice nurses were small. Stilwell (1982) emphasised the importance of a screening and health education component of the nurse practitioner/patient consultation.

MacGuire (1980) argued that, in the United Kingdom:

'Nurses here are quietly expanding their roles... to meet new demands without an accompanying fanfare of new titles. Let us not be misled into thinking that in adopting "nurse practitioners" we would be introducing anything new.'

One of the recommendations of the Cumberlege Review Committee, reporting on community nursing, was that community nurses should be encouraged to develop their role into that of nurse practitioners, providing support, health education and early detection of problems, and caring for those with chronic diseases (Department of Health and Social Security, 1986).

The Cumberlege Review Committee recommended that privately employed practice nurses should be phased out by the withdrawal of their salary reimbursement to general practitioners. The objections to this role were both economic and professional. The latter included a dislike of the control of nurses by other professions, and the lack of appropriate training and nursing support. Concern about the role of the practice nurse had been expressed previously (Hockey, 1984).

The practice nurse's role has become a controversial issue and has been debated extensively. The need to further describe and define their role was evident before the report of the Cumberlege Review Committee was published. The authors of this chapter also felt it was necessary to ascertain the reasons why some general practitioners employed nurses, and to pinpoint the factors responsible for variations in the nurse's role.

Aims of the study

The first part of the study was designed to:

1   Collect demographic details of nurses employed in general practice;
2   Identify their duties and responsibilities;
3   Ascertain their views on the training they had already received and further training that they feel they may require;
4   Enquire about their opinions and attitudes towards possible extensions to their role.

Study design

The Royal College of Nursing (1984) defined a practice nurse as:

'A Registered General Nurse who is employed by the general practitioner to work within the treatment room and is a member of the team responsible for clinical care of the practice population together with the district nursing team of the health authority.'

The definition of practice nurses used in this study included every nurse who was employed by the general practitioner, and had the word 'nurse' in his/her title (for example, nurse/receptionist or enrolled nurse).

Practice nurses are not the only nurses who work in the surgery or treatment room of general practices; nurses employed by health authorities may do so (and are sometimes confusingly referred to as practice nurses). To examine the role of privately employed practice nurses in isolation seemed too limited. It was thus thought that the health authority nurses would provide a useful yardstick with which to compare and contrast the 'practice nurse's' role. Therefore, when the study was being planned, provisions were made for the health authority employed nurses to be included.

The nurses employed by the health authority formed two groups: treatment room nurses and district nurses. The term 'treatment room nurse' was reserved for nurses who worked exclusively in the treatment rooms of health centres or general practitioners' surgeries (not all health authorities provide this post). The 'district nurse' group included any nurse employed as such, with or without the district nurse qualification, who was a registered general or enrolled nurse. Some district nurses also worked for part of their time in surgeries and treatment rooms.

The sample

Nottinghamshire was selected as the study area because it was conveniently organised by one family practitioner committee and covered three health authorities with varying sociogeographic characteristics. The number of nurses working in the general practices within this area (serving a population of approximately one million) was thought to be sufficiently large to provide an adequate sample for the study, and to allow for some generalisations to be made.

There were some problems with identifying the number and location of practice nurses accurately, as initially details from the family practitioner committee offices were found to be incomplete, and often out of date. The information regarding treatment room nurses and district nurses was obtained from health authorities.

All practice nurses (n = 79) and treatment room nurses (n = 18) were included. A representative subsample of district nurses was taken. The sample consisted of those nurses who had undertaken surgery duties during one particular week in February 1986 (n =71).

In Nottinghamshire, 226 general practice bases were identified. A base was defined as an address from which a practice operated. There were several bases at a health centre if practices within them were independent, and some practices had two or more surgery premises. The nursing provision is shown in Table 9.1. Usually only one type of nurse worked at a base, but at 12% of bases combinations of nurses were found. Just over one-third of practice bases within the study area did not have a nurse working on the premises. The 79 practice nurses worked at 61 bases (27.0%) between them; the 18 treatment room nurses treated patients from 55 practice bases (24.3%); and the district nurses held surgery sessions at 59 bases (26.1%).

Response rate

The response rate (calculated as one or more nurses responding from a base) was

100% for the treatment room nurses, 93% for those bases with district nurses, and 77% for bases employing practice nurses.

Table 9.1   Nursing provision – practices in Nottinghamshire

	Number of practice bases	% of bases with type of nurses
Practice nurse only	43	19.0
Treatment room nurse only	37	16.4
District nurse only	38	16.8
Practice and treatment room nurse	7	3.1
Practice and district nurse	10	4.4
Treatment room and district nurse	10	4.4
Practice, treatment room and district nurse	1	0.4
None	80	35.4
	226	

Research method

The method selected to collect data for the first descriptive phase of the study was that of a postal questionnaire. A method of analysis was employed that enabled a comparison to be made of nurses who worked for different numbers of hours each week. Relative frequency was used as the method of comparison; that is the interval between carrying out certain tasks, rather than the number of times a task was performed, was the basis for calculation. Nurses were asked how regularly they carried out certain duties – regularly (meaning daily or weekly), occasionally (less than once a week but each month), rarely (less than once each month) or never (not carried out this duty). Thus, whether they carried out a specific task regularly or not could be ascertained.

Results

Nurses' duties

All the treatment room nurses said that they syringed ears regularly, as did 84% of district nurses and 75% of practice nurses. Ten (18%) of the practice nurses never syringed ears. From this (for each nurse group) a group habitual score was calculated. This gave a weighting of 3 to 'regularly', 2 to 'occasionally', 1 to 'rarely' and 0 to 'never'. The practice nurses scored 2.4, the treatment room nurses 3, and district nurses 2.8.

The scores were calculated for each duty/task listed in the questionnaire. This provided a basis for summarising the numerous results and allowed comparison to be made between both the individual nurses and the different categories of nurses in relation to the type and frequency of the nursing duties they performed.

The 25% highest scoring duties for each group of nurses (i.e. the ones they did most regularly) are listed in Table 9.2. Shown first are eight items common to all groups. These are traditionally considered to be nurses' duties.

Table 9.2 Group habitual score: 25% most regularly recorded duties

All nurses	Practice nurse/ treatment room nurse	Treatment room nurse/district nurse only
Dressings	Immunisation (travel and flu)	Venepuncture
Injections		Collect MSU
Suture removal		Order stock
Ear syringing		Maintain equipment
Advice/information		
Listening	*Practice nurses only*	*District nurses only*
Urinalysis	Weight/height	Counselling
Reception of casual	Blood pressure	
attenders and emergencies	Chaperon	Temperature, pulse,
	Telephone advice	respiration rate

The ranking order was different between the groups of nurses. For example, ear syringing and suture removal were equally the highest scoring duties for treatment room and district nurses, but ear syringing was ranked eighth and suture removal 11th for practice nurses.

Both practice and treatment room nurses included immunisation for travellers and prevention of 'flu among their top 25% tasks. In addition, practice nurses scored higher on weighing patients, recording blood pressure, chaperoning and giving telephone advice. Both groups of health authority employed nurses included venepuncture, collection of midstream specimens of urine (MSU), ordering treatment room stock and maintaining equipment in their top 25% most regularly performed tasks (venepuncture ranked 17th for practice nurses). Among the duties most regularly undertaken by the district nurses were counselling and recording of temperature, pulse and respiration rates.

Nurses were also asked to record any additional duties they did which were not included in the questionnaire. The most frequently mentioned additional duty listed by the practice nurses was responsibility for organising some type of call and recall system for patients. None of the other nurses reported doing this. Several health authority nurses added that they arranged home equipment loans and issued materials for use in the management of incontinence.

One of the other tasks recorded by the practice nurses was cleaning. Three of the practice nurses (5%) reported that they cleaned the surgery; two at the same practice doing this weekly, the other nurse 'rarely'. A study by the Cornwall and Isles of Scilly Family Practitioner Committee (1986) reported that 30% of practice nurses undertook some cleaning duties (although these were not defined) (*Nursing Times*, 1986).

Of the practice nurses, 25% made visits to patients' homes regularly (every week); the main single reason given was to carry out procedures that the district nurses were not permitted to do or were unable to do (for example, to give vaccinations to prevent 'flu, venepuncture, and to record electrocardiograms).

If all reasons related to assessment are combined (observations and investigations, follow-up after a doctor's visit or assessment/surveillance of the elderly, and assessment of the need for a doctor to visit), assessment was the most frequent reason given by practice nurses for home visiting.

The nurse's role in preventive medicine: selected results

The current trend in general practice is to give more emphasis to prevention of disease (Fowler, 1982). This may have altered the nurse's role away from a concern with illness and treatments towards dealing with healthy individuals and promoting health.

Preventive care, as Fowler states, can be divided into three stages: primary, secondary and tertiary prevention. Primary prevention involves identifying risk factors and removing the cause (for example, education to prevent/reduce unhealthy behaviour). Secondary prevention is concerned with the early detection of disease before symptoms appear (screening), and tertiary prevention is the management of established disease to avoid or limit the development of further disability (supervision of people with chronic conditions).

Primary prevention Before giving advice to modify tobacco consumption or reduce obesity, these and other *risk factors* need identifying by questioning patients about smoking habits, alcohol consumption, family histories and recording of weight. General practitioners and/or nurses may be involved in this assessment.

Risk factor identification was a regular feature of the work of nearly a quarter of practice and treatment room nurses, and of 8% of the district nurses. It was reported as an occasional feature by 21% of practice nurses, 11% of treatment room nurses and 13% of district nurses.

More practice nurses than treatment room or district nurses replied that weighing patients and measuring height were regular features of their work. Seven per cent of practice nurses, 28% of treatment room nurses and more than 36% of district nurses stated that they *never* weighed patients.

The nurses' involvement in giving advice and guidance about *diet*, after they (or the general practitioner) had identified obesity, showed that a smaller proportion were actively attempting to follow-up and modify this risk after its identification. Asked if they tried to help patients to lose weight either in normal surgery sessions or specially arranged clinics, many more of the practice nurses replied that they did so: 34% compared with 5% of treatment room nurses and 2% of district nurses.

One in four of the practice nurses, about 1 in 10 of the treatment room nurses, and 1 in 14 of the district nurses indicated that they regularly (at least once a week) advised a patient about giving up *smoking*.

Secondary prevention   The numbers of nurses involved in aspects of *screening* are given in Table 9.3. Screening for hypertension may be initiated by nurses themselves: it may be done on an opportunistic basis, or as part of a planned programme. The percentage of practice nurses who reported that they screened patients for hypertension was higher (41%) than that of the treatment room nurses (22%). The percentage of district nurses was lowest (12%).

Table 9.3   Involvement with screening

	Hypertension	Well woman	Well man
Practice nurses (n = 56)	23 41.1%	28 50.0%	5 8.9%
Treatment room nurses (n = 18)	4 22.2%	0	0
District nurses (n = 57)	7 12.3%	3 5.3%	3 5.3%

χ^2 PN/TRN Not significant $P<0.001$
    PN/DN $P<0.001$ $P<0.001$

The nurses' involvement with other screening programmes ('well woman' or 'well man' clinics) is also shown in Table 9.3.

Breast self-examination is one item that may be taught or discussed at a 'well woman clinic'. Fewer nurses gave instruction about breast examination than they did about screening for hypertension, but the same pattern was found between the groups of nurses. Thirty-four per cent of practice nurses carried this out at least once a week, compared to 5% of both treatment room and district nurses. A further 21% of practice nurses carried this out occasionally, in comparison with 11% of treatment room nurses and 14% of district nurses. The remainder performed this rarely or never.

Less than half (46%) of the practice nurses answered that they took *cervical smears* regularly; a further 11% did this rarely (less than once each month), and 43% said they never took smears. The number of treatment room nurses and district nurses who never took cervical smears for cytology was 79% and 90% respectively.

Tertiary prevention   Nurses have been involved in caring for patients with chronic diseases such as diabetes, hypertension and asthma. Table 9.4 shows that practice nurses were more likely to have responsibility for such care, with the exception of diabetes where a greater proportion of the district nurses are involved (e.g. in giving insulin injections and management of care).

In the provision of care for people with chronic illnesses, nurses may be making clinical assessments, offering advice to and educating patients to enable them to understand and manage their conditions, or they may merely record observations from which the general practitioner may make decisions.

Table 9.4   Tertiary prevention: proportion of nurses delegated responsibility for care, assessment and management/supervision of patients with a chronic illness

	Practice nurses %	Treatment room nurses %	District nurses %
Hypertension (x^2: $P<0.01$ DN vs PN)	59	53	33
Diabetes (not statistically significant)	43	37	53
Asthma (x^2: $P<0.01$ DN vs PN)	32	16	12

Extent of nurses' responsibilities

It is difficult to assess the amount of responsibility and decision making given to, or accepted by, nurses when they undertake a procedure. Several attempts to estimate this were made. One way was to ask the nurses to report their own estimation of their level of responsibility.

Fewer district nurses (11%) felt that they had high levels of responsibility or took much part in decision making. Altogether 49% of the district nurses felt that they had high or moderate levels of responsibility in comparison with three quarters of the practice nurses, and 58% of the treatment room nurses. More of the district nurses reported that there was little responsibility or decision making in their work (16%, in comparison with 6% of practice nurses and 5% of treatment room nurses). The remainder felt they had 'some' responsibility and decision making power (x^2 practice nurses when compared with district nurses, $P<0.001$).

The level of responsibility assigned for one task only was assessed using ear syringing as the example. In the questionnaire, two levels of decision making and responsibility for this procedure were given. Nurses were asked to choose which was the nearest to their own practice. The examples were:

1   A patient is referred to you by the general practitioner to have his ears syringed. The general practitioner has diagnosed the problem, prescribed necessary wax softening agents and decided to delegate the ear syringing procedure to you.

2   A patient requests (or is directed by the receptionist to you) to have his ears syringed. You obtain a history of his complaint, examine his ears and assess if wax is present, then elicit any contraindications. You recommend softening agents if required. You decide (based on your judgement) that syringing is required and you carry out this procedure without obtaining specific permission because there is agreement that this is delegated to you.

The results are shown in Table 9.5.

Table 9.5   Ear syringing

Nurses who syringe ears only	GP refers patients	Nurse assesses need/ contraindications, carries out procedure	Both apply
Practice nurses (n = 46)	18 39.1%	20 43.5%	8 17.4%
Treatment room nurses (n = 18)	14 77.8%	4 22.2%	
District nurses (n = 55)	50 90.9%	3 5.5%	2 3.6%

χ^2: PN/TRN $P<0.01$; PN/DN $P<0.0001$

Increased responsibility may be demonstrated when patients are allowed direct or open access to the nurse (i.e. they could request to see the nurse for treatment or advice without reference to the general practitioner). Patients had direct access to all the treatment room nurses in the survey, all but two of the practice nurses (96%), and 71% of the district nurses.

Nurse practitioner role

Nurses were asked if they thought that they had extended their role towards that of a nurse practitioner. It was suggested that the range of nurses' duties and responsibilities could be conceived as a continuum. At one extreme was a nurse with a role limited to carrying out only delegated tasks, and at the opposite end was a nurse practitioner who was encouraged to take on additional responsibilities, and was available for patients to consult for a range of treatments, assessments or advice without necessarily seeing a general practitioner first. A visual analogue scale was presented. Not everyone would agree with this conception. Fawcett-Henesy is reported as saying 'there is no way you can become a nurse practitioner without training' (*General Practitioner*, 1986).

The majority of each of the groups thought that they had made little progress towards the role of a nurse practitioner (indicated by placing a mark on the first third of the analogue scale). Between 21% and 32% thought they had extended their role some distance towards that of nurse practitioners (the final third of the scale) – see Table 9.6.

Nurses were asked if they would like an opportunity to develop their role towards that of a nurse practitioner. The results from this enquiry were combined for all three groups of nurses, as there were no differences between them, and are shown in Table 9.7. The percentages on the left apply to those who perceived a little or no extension to their roles. They had marked the analogue scale less than half way across. The percentages on the right relate to the nurses who considered their role to be towards that of a nurse practitioner (over half way across the continuum). More of the nurses who perceived that their role was nearer to that of a nurse practitioner (53%) replied that they would wish to extend their role still further. Overall, 39% of the nurses sampled would like to extend or develop their roles in this way.

Table 9.6   Self-reported extension towards nurse practitioner role

	Nurse		Nurse practitioner
Practice nurses ($n = 54$)	26 48.1%	11 20.4%	17 31.5%
Treatment room nurses ($n = 19$)	9 47.4%	5 26.3%	5 26.3%
District nurses ($n = 57$)	36 63.2%	9 15.8%	12 21.1%

Mann–Whitney U Test, not significant

Table 9.7   Wish for opportunity to extend or develop further towards a nurse practitioner role

	Self-perceived extent of nurse practitioner role		
	Nurse		Nurse practitioner
	$n = 85$	$n = 38$	
Yes	33%	53%	
No	29%	8%	
Not sure	38%	18%	
Not applicable, already nurse practitioner	—	21%	

χ^2: $P < 0.001$

Summary

Nurses working in general practice have reported on the work they do and have given information on whether or not they wish to extend their roles towards that of a nurse practitioner. The questionnaire was also designed to identify the training they had received and their views on their further educational needs. Whilst this chapter has been restricted to the former question, training is an important consideration because extending the nurse's role seems to be linked with opportunities to learn.

From the nurses' reports, it became apparent that those who worked solely in practices have become involved in a wider range of duties and responsibilities than the district nurses (irrespective of who employed them). Practice nurses listed 'preventive' services more frequently in the description of their work than did the health authority employed nurses. The preventive work performed by the practice nurses was not solely confined to those areas that attract item-of-service payments for the general practitioner. Health promotion and screening are developing areas in general practice and this appears to be the area in which practice nurses are developing their role.

The district nurses' work in the practice was mainly confined to undertaking dressings or giving injections, which they would otherwise have done in patients' homes. In addition, they undertook ear syringing and venepuncture. The district nurse's main role is caring for the sick in their homes. In recent years, there has been an increase in the numbers of elderly people in the community. Patients are discharged earlier from hospital and the trend is towards community rather than institutional care. To expect district nurses to expand their role even further by undertaking more preventive work and acting as a nurse practitioner is perhaps too much to ask.

The amount of work a nurse carries out is limited both by the time spent at the surgery and by the size of the practice population. Data from the study showed that practice nurses worked, on average, 9.7 hours per week per general practitioner. The treatment room nurses' allocation was 2.9 hours, and the district nurses' time spent at the surgery averaged 1.3 hours per week per general practitioner.

It has been shown that treatments and investigations featured highly for the two groups of nurses. Whilst opportunistic screening or health promotion can be undertaken together with treatments the evidence did not show that this happens. The explanation could be that preventive care may be seen as the province of other members of the primary health care team, for example the general practitioner or the health visitor. It may not be recognised as necessary by others. If preventive medicine is to develop further, as has been suggested, perhaps the surgery-based nurses are in the strongest position to adapt their role to that end. The project continues: it is hoped that further work will clarify these roles.

Acknowledgements

We are indebted to Trent Regional Health Authority who funded this project through a Regional Research Committee grant. Thanks are also extended to the nurses who responded to our invitation to participate in the study.

References

Allen P (1976) Too many elderly patients to care for? *Modern Geriatrics*, **6**, 15–17
Bain D G J & Haines A J (1974) A treatment room survey in a health centre in a new town. *Health Bulletin*, **32**, 111–119

Baldwin J T (1967) The use of a nurse in general practice. *Journal of the Royal College of General Practitioners*, **13**, 364–367

Bowling A (1981a) Delegation to nurses in general practice. *Journal of the Royal College of General Practitioners*, **31**, 485–490

Bowling A (1981b) *Delegation in General Practice. A Study of Doctors and Nurses*. London: Tavistock Publications

Carroll-Williams B & Allen J (1984) Running a well man clinic. *Nursing Times*, **80**, 34–35

Cartwright A & Scott R (1961) The work of a nurse employed in general practice. *British Medical Journal*, **i**, 807–813

Cornwall and Isles of Scilly Family Practitioner Committee (1986) *A Research Study into the Provision, Distribution and Use of Practice Nurses in Cornwall*. Cornwall: Cornwall and Isles of Scilly Family Practitioner Committee

Deans W & Hoskins R (1987) The Castlemilk well-man clinic. In *Coronary Heart Disease – Reducing the Risk. Chichester: Wiley/Open University*

Department of Health and Social Security (1986) Neighbourhood Nursing – a Focus for Care. Report of the Community Nursing Review (Cumberlege Report). London: HMSO

Diamond M (1986) Ploughing back the profits. *Nursing Times*, **82**, 44–45

Dixon P N (1969) Work of a nurse in a health centre treatment room. *British Medical Journal*, **4**, 292–294

Dopson L (1984) Down your way – practice nurses. *Nursing Times*, **80**, 33

Doyle C (1987) A new tonic at the doctors. *The Daily Telegraph*, 14 April, 11

Dunnell K & Dobbs J (1980) *Nurses Working in the Community*. London: HMSO

Fowler G (1982) Prevention – what does it mean? *British Medical Journal*, **284**, 945–946

Fullard E, Fowler G & Gray M (1984) Facilitating prevention in primary care. *British Medical Journal*, **289**, 1585–1587

Goddard B (1981) Present practice. Clinical forum 8 – practice nurses and GPs. *Nursing Mirror*, Supplement, 19 August, x-xi

General Practitioner (1986) News: most practice nurses are not nurse practitioners. *General Practitioner*, 31 October

Hall C (1982) Nurse with a stethoscope. *World Medicine*, 16 October, 75–77

Hart J T (1985) Practice nurses: an underused resource. *British Medical Journal*, **290**, 1162–1163

Hockey L (1972) *Use or Abuse – a Study of State Enrolled Nurse in the Local Authority Nursing*. London: Queen's Institute of District Nursing

Hockey L (1984) Is the practice nurse a good idea? *Journal of the Royal College of General Practitioners*, **34**, 102–103

Hodgkin K & Gillie C (1968) Relieving the strain by work study and a practice nurse in a two-doctor urban practice. *Journal of the Royal College of General Practitioners*, Reports for general practice, 10. London: Royal College of General Practitioners

Hudson M (1985) Our team's approach to mild hypertension management. *Pulse*, 16 November, 51–53

Laurance J (1985) Practice nurses can be a boon. *General Practitioner*, 14 June, 46

MacGuire J M (1980) *The Expanded Role of the Nurse*. London: King's Fund Centre

McIntosh J B (1979) Making the best use of time. *Nursing Mirror*, **149**, 32–33

Marriott R G (1981) Open access to the practice nurse. *Journal of the Royal College of General Practitioners*, **31**, 235–238

Marsh G N (1967) Group practice nurse: an analysis and comment on six months' work. *British Medical Journal*, **1**, 489–491

Marsh G N (1976) Further nursing care in general practice. *British Medical Journal*, **2**, 626–627

Marsh G N (1978) Are we making the best use of nurses? *Modern Medicine*, **23**, 30–34

Marsh G N (1985) More nurses needed. *Nursing Times Community Outlook*, **81**, 10–11

Marsh G N & Chew C (1984) Well man clinic in general practice. *British Medical Journal*, **288**, 200–201

Mottram E (1968) Extended use of nursing services in general practice. *Nursing Mirror*, **126**, 20–24

Murray J (1967) Fifteen years in general practice. *Journal of the Royal College of General Practitioners*, **13**, 367

Nimmo A W (1978a) Treatment room work: an analysis. *Nursing Times*, **74**, 109–112

Nimmo A W (1978b) Treatment room work: an analysis – 2. *Nursing Times*, **74**, 113–116

Nursing Times (1986) News: practice nurses brush up on cleaning skills. *Nursing Times*, **82**, 5

Pearson R (1985) Asthma clinic success story. *Pulse*, 8 June, 59

Powell R A (1984) The practice nurse – a review. *Journal of the Royal College of General Practitioners*, **34**, 100–101

Pownall M (1985) Action men, *Nursing Times*, **81**, 16–17

Reedy B L E C (1972a) Organisation and management: the general practice nurse. *Update*, **5**, 336–370

Reedy B L E C (1972b) Organisation and management: the general practice nurse. *Update*, **5**, 187–193

Reedy B L E C, Metcalfe A V, de Roumanie M & Newell D J (1980a) The social and occupational characteristics of attached and employed nurses in general practice. *Journal of the Royal College of General Practitioners*, **30**, 477–482

Reedy B L E C , Metcalfe A V, de Roumanie M & Newell D J (1980b) A comparison of the activities and opinions of attached and employed nurses in general practice. *Journal of the Royal College of General Practitioners*, **30**, 483–489

Royal College of Nursing (1984) *Training Needs of Practice Nurses*. London: Royal College of Nursing

Smith E & Bignell L (1987) Diabetic support clinic. *Primary Health Care*, January, 4

Stilwell B (1982) The nurse practitioner at work. 1. Primary Care. *Nursing Times*, **78**, 1799–1803

Stilwell B (1984) the nurse in practice. *Nursing Mirror*, **158**, 17–19

Vousden M (1985) Wise council. *Nursing Mirror*, **160**, 46–48

Walters W H R, Sandeman J M & Lunn J E (1980) A four year prospective study of the work of the practice nurse in the treatment room of a South Yorkshire practice. *British Medical Journal*, **280**, 87–89

Weston Smith J & O'Donovan J B (1970) The practice nurse – a new look. *British Medical Journal*, **4**, 673–677

10
Patients' Attitudes to the Availability of a Nurse Practitioner in General Practice

BARBARA STILWELL

As described in Chapter 6, from 1982 to 1985 a nurse practitioner was available for patients to consult in an inner city general practice in Birmingham. The evaluation of this experiment included a questionnaire for patients which elicited their views on the introduction of a nurse practitioner into the practice. The results of this enquiry are the subject of this chapter.

The Practice

There were 4728 patients, of whom 49% were female, registered with two male doctors (one of these was joined in 1983 by a female partner) practising separately from joint premises. The practice was situated in an inner city area where unemployment was high and wages for those in employment were low.

There was no appointment system in either practice. Patients of the two-doctor partnership were required to attend between 8 a.m. and 9 a.m. The third doctor had a later morning surgery from 9.30 a.m. to 10.30 a.m. Evening surgery ran from 4.30 p.m. to 6 p.m. for all doctors.

The nurse practitioner worked with all three doctors, seeing most patients on the premises, rather than during home visits. A large notice in the waiting room informed patients that a nurse practitioner was available:

'A nurse practitioner is now working in this surgery. She is a nurse and a health visitor who has had extra training in looking after common family health problems. If you would like to see the nurse practitioner please tell the receptionist.'

Patient questionnaire

Two years after this service had been initiated a random sample of 235 patients aged 16 and over (about 5% of the practice) was drawn from the age–sex registers. Forty per cent were found to have died or moved, or were untraceable in the practice records, leaving 140 who were sent postal questionnaires. This sought their opinion on the availability of a nurse practitioner and their satisfaction with any consultations they had with her, asked about the qualities they expected in health care professionals, and assured them that replies would be treated confidentially.

Ninety per cent of patients (126) returned the postal questionnaire, of whom 54% were female.

Patients' attitudes

The majority (82%) of patients were born in the UK, although a quarter had at least one parent born elsewhere.

Patients were asked to give their occupation: all did so, and the social class grouping of their occupations is given in Table 10.1. The social class of patients consulting the nurse practitioner is also compared in the table with that of the ward population.

Table 10.1 Social class of 125 economically active persons from the practice who consulted the nurse practitioner compared with the ward population from the 1981 Census

Social class grouping	% of patients from practice	% ward population
I	0.8	2.8
II	20.8	18.6
III (N)	35.2	24.5
III (M)	27.2	24.9
IV	9.6	18.4
V	6.4	5.1
Armed forces and inadequately described	—	5.3

Ninety-two patients explained what they thought the nurse practitioner did and described different aspects of her role: those mentioned most frequently are listed in Table 10.2. Some patients perceived the nurse practitioner as having an advisory or supportive function as well as saving the doctors' time by performing practical tasks.

Table 10.2

What patients thought the nurse practitioner did	No. of patients (n = 92)	As a percentage
Helps the doctor	49	38.8
Treats minor ailments	24	19
Practical tasks	20	15.8
Gives advice	18	14.2
Preventive medicine	10	7.9
Treats specific groups (e.g. women, children)	9	7.1
Does the same as the doctor	9	7.1
Non-medical tasks	5	3.9
Counselling	4	3.1
Doesn't prescribe	3	2.3

The following selection of respondents' comments illustates these points:

F   *School Secretary*
'Takes work from doctors shoulders when advice is needed more than medication. She is also capable of taking BPs, smears, etc., to save the doctors' time for more urgent needs.'

F   *Tester of Gas Appliances*
'Helps by listening to a person's problems and would suggest seeing a doctor when necessary.'

F   *Housewife*
'Takes the workload off the doctor and is able to spend more time with individual patients.'

Other people thought nurse practitioner care suitable for particular groups of patients, thus:

M   *Foreman Sign Maker*
'Shares workload with doctor by helping with personal problems, dressings, stitches, etc. Helpful with young mothers or elderly.'

F   *Retired*
'...I thought she was for women's ailments and children.'

Fifty-eight respondents (46%) felt there was a difference between the nurse practitioner's and the doctor's roles. Fifty-four people said what they thought the differences were and those most frequently mentioned are listed in Table 10.3. Sixty-one patients had visited the nurse practitioner at least once; their reasons for choosing to see her rather than the doctor included the nature of their illness (mentioned 13 times), the personal qualities of the nurse practitioner (mentioned 12 times), to save time, and personal reasons (each mentioned twice). Ten patients said that they did not choose to see the nurse practitioner, indicating perhaps that they were referred by someone else, or that they had been persuaded to do so by a receptionist. However, most people chose to consult the nurse practitioner about problems that were non-clinical, such as preventive procedures, health education and social or emotional concerns, thus:

F   *Word Processor Operator*
     'I chose to see the nurse practitioner because I had a personal problem and needed someone to talk to.'
F   *Unemployed*
     'Because I feel that I can easily express my illness to her without feeling embarassed. She also explains your illness, if it's good or bad news.'

Table 10.3

What patients thought was the difference between nurse practitioner and doctor	No. of patients (58)	Percentage
Qualifications	23	39.6
Ability to prescribe	21	36.2
The type of complaints they deal with	16	12.6
Authority	11	8.7
Ability to diagnose	11	8.7
Personal qualities	8	6.3
Knowledge	6	4.7
Ability to refer to consultants	4	3.1

In response to a question asking if it would make any difference if the nurse practitioner were a man there were 25 answers from 21 women and 4 men. Two men said that they would prefer to see a doctor, one that a male nurse practitioner would have 'a different personality' and one that for religious reasons he had to have someone of the same sex examine him.

All the female respondents preferred a female nurse practitioner:

F   *Housewife*
'If you are a woman I think they understand you and you are more relaxed. They seem to know when you explain your problems.'
F   *Office Junior*
'I would be able to relate to a woman about certain things more easily than a man.'

Of the 61 people who had visited the nurse practitioner 36 (59%) said they would consult her again, four would not and 19 did not know (there were two non-responders).

Some reasons given by those willing to consult the nurse practitioner again were:

F   *Unemployed*
'Because she generally seems interested in you, does not seem to treat you with the attitude that she has heard it all before. She also takes time to explain what she is doing and why, for example she told me all about a smear whereas the doctor did not.'
F   *Housewife and Part-time Cleaner*
'Our doctor is *very* good and always listens before deciding what to do. But some problems do not need medication. Sometimes you just need advice or just someone to listen. When there is not anything physically wrong you feel one probably has more time to listen. You are not taking the time up of the doctor, who can deal with more urgent cases.'
F   *Housewife and Mother*
'Because she seems to listen, has more time and you don't feel so self-conscious.'

Patients were asked whether there were any problems about which they would prefer to see a nurse practitioner. Fifty-nine (47%) said there were not, 26 (21%) said there were, 21 (17%) did not know and 20 (15%) gave no response. The problems patients preferred to see a nurse about are listed in Table 10.4.

Forty-seven patients said they would prefer to see a doctor for certain problems, and 34 patients (27%) would not. Eighteen (14%) patients did not know and there were 27 (22%) non-responders. Both questions about the preferred practitioner elicited a high proportion of uncertain replies, either in terms of non-responders or those who did not know.

When asked whether having a nurse practitioner at the doctors' surgery was a good idea, 95 patients responded. Ninety-one (96%) thought it was a good idea, four (4.2%) thought it was not, and one person did not know. When asked why it was a good idea patients most often said because it saved the doctor's time or relieved him or her of trivial and routine matters (mentioned by 54.7% of respondents). Improving the smooth running of the surgery by cutting down waiting time was mentioned by 13.6% of patients. Other reasons given were having a choice of practitioners (six people), having a female available to consult (six people) and the style of the nurse practitioner's consultations (12 people).

Table 10.4   26 patients mentioned 70 problems about which they would prefer to consult a nurse

Diagnostic group	No. of times mentioned
Infections and parasitic diseases	3
Mental disorders	4
Diseases of the nervous system and sense organs	2
Diseases of the respiratory system	3
Diseases of the digestive system	1
Diseases of the genitourinary system	4
Pregnancy, childbirth and the puerperium	2
Disease of the skin and subcutaneous tissue	4
Symptoms, signs and ill-defined conditions	2
Accidents, injuries, poisoning and violence	1
Supplementary classification	44

Typical responses included these:

F   *Office Junior*
'It helps the doctor, and some women prefer to see a woman about their complaint.'
F   *Unemployed*
'Sometimes when I go with trivial things I think I am wasting the doctor's time. She doesn't seem to mind how small the trouble.'
M   *Self-employed Sign Erector*
'People's needs are different and many types of treatment, etc., do not require a doctor's skill.'

This was a small sample of patients, whose views were elicited to complement other aspects of an evaluation of the nurse practitioner role in general practice. As such, it is of limited value, but serves to indicate aspects of nursing that are particularly useful for patients in ambulatory care. Certain trends in the results of this small sample are similar to those in other larger studies, which will be discussed, suggesting that the opinions expressed by respondents in this study may be representative of a common view.

Discussion

The majority of people who had consulted the nurse practitioner expressed a willingness to do so again, implying satisfaction with their experience of nurse practitioner care. This finding mirrors American studies that have evaluated patient satisfaction with nurse practitioner care. Lewis and Resnick (1967) carried out one of the early studies of satisfaction with nursing care amongst patients attending a clinic for the chronically sick. They found that after one year of nurse practitioner care patients showed a significant increase in preference for nursing care. They questioned 66 patients about the work of one nurse practitioner.

However, Levine and colleagues (1978) questioned 700 patients who had been cared for by 58 nurse practitioners working in a variety of settings. A high level of satisfaction was found among this sample of patients, over 90% of them rating the nurse practitioner as good or very good. This is a reassuringly large sample, which confirms the findings of smaller studies, including the Birmingham project described here.

Hogan and Hogan (1982) analysed questionnaires from 1223 employees of Illinois State University which elicited their attitudes to various aspects of care that could be undertaken by a nurse practitioner. They found that there was a greater level of acceptance of traditional nursing roles than the extended nurse practitioner role among those people who had not previously consulted a nurse practitioner. Those respondents who had previously consulted a nurse practitioner reported a 90% satisfaction rate with their treatment. This accords with the Birmingham study in which only 12% of those who had not consulted the nurse practitioner thought that they would do so in the future, and 31% thought that they would not.

The reasons why people would consult the nurse practitioner again were generally concerned with the non-practical aspects of her work: these included the time she spent with people, listening and making people feel at ease.

Reedy (1972) refers to the work of practice nurses as counsellors, listeners and advisers as work created for them by patients. He says:

> 'It is the common experience of practice nurses that patients see them as being more accessible than the doctor and easier to communicate with. They build up an informal relationship with the nurse which tends to allow and encourage unscheduled consultations with her, and as the depth of this relationship increases with time and extends to include more and more patients ...she is increasingly used as the point of first contact in the surgery.'

Although in the Birmingham study the nurse had an extended role , patients still tended to view her as being more accessible than the doctors, and easier to talk to. This attitude to nurses may reflect Anderson's (1973) finding that nurses were expected by the public to be kind and sympathetic. On the other hand, Gray (1982) puts a case for 'femaleness' (that is, warmth, caring and sympathy) improving the quality and outcomes of consultations for many patients, particularly women. Oakley (1984) discusses the sex division between medicine and nursing not only in terms of doctors being men and nurses women, but in terms of medicine espousing masculine values. Doctors, male and female, are, she says 'rational, scientific, unemotional and uninvolved: indeed, their very value is sometimes said to lie in their detachment from the personal needs of their patients.' It may be for this reason that people perceive nurses as more suitable counsellors and as more approachable than doctors.

Hull and Hull (1984) have noted from a sample of 1112 patients that many were dissatisfied with the time given to them by their general practitioners. In particular, they note that nearly half of women interviewed who were between the ages of 15 and 44 found that they had difficulty in telling the doctor why they had attended. The Birmingham study revealed that women were nearly three times as likely as men to say there were problems for which they would prefer to consult a nurse practitioner. This may simply indicate a sex preference or it may be an expression of some women's search for a more 'female' style of care.

Cartwright and Anderson (1981) found in their 1977 survey of patients and doctors that the proportion of patients who thought their general practitioner a suitable person to talk to about family problems had declined from 40% in a (similar) survey of 10 years previously to 30%. Less than a third of patients, in both surveys, said they would turn to their general practitioners for help with a personal problem. Discussing family and personal problems constituted a large part of the nurse practitioner's work in the Birmingham study: nurses may be more appropriate care givers in these situations.

A number of respondents to the Birmingham questionnaire mentioned that the nurse practitioner treated them as an individual or that it did not seem to them that 'she'd heard it all before'. Undoubtedly, the amount of time the nurse practitioner gave to each consultation influenced these patients' perceptions, allowing, as it did, the opportunity for a relationship to develop between practitioner and patient. Lewis and Resnick (1967) reflect that their positive results about nursing may be a result of a placebo effect. They say:

> 'It seems reasonable that patients provided [with] a continuing relationship with anyone ...exhibiting an interest in them would be satisfied and "do better", at least for a time.'

Eisenberg (1977) comments on a similar phenomenon in doctors' consultations. He suggests that the mere presence of a doctor is a medicine in itself, because the physician is believed to possess 'special prerogatives in sanctioning illness and arcane skills in restoring health': the physician retains some qualities of 'magic'. He goes on to say that the doctor's task ought to be to educate patients to help them to understand the nature of illness and its cure, so that they can begin to make educated decisions about their own health. The process is one of demystifying medicine. Could nurse practitioners meet patients' needs for sympathetic concern, assist them to understand and manage their own health and have a 'magical effect'?

It is not yet possible to answer the last question, but outcome studies *have* shown that patients being cared for by nurse practitioners keep appointments, lose weight effectively, quit smoking more frequently and experience fewer symptoms (Ramsay et al, 1982; Watkins & Wagner 1982; Kenkre et al, 1985). Levine and colleagues (1978) found in their study of nurse practitioner care that patients appreciated the average consultation time of 22 minutes. Patients commented that:

> 'she did not appear rushed, answered questions adequately, was reassuring, made the patient or the parent of the patient feel he was in good hands, was able to

understand the medical problem of both adult and paediatric patients and did not make the patient self-conscious about asking "silly questions".'

Comments from patients in the Birmingham nurse practitioner study often related to being treated by the nurse practitioner as an individual, being able to explain their illness without feeling embarrassed, and being able to ask questions. Adopting a style of consultation that allows patients to feel able to participate may also facilitate learning for patients and encourage 'self-responsibility' for health. This may threaten the 'magic' of medicine by demystifying it; there may be compensations for the patient in terms of increased self-reliance and control.

Studies of nurse practitioner care have been slow to examine the process behind the outcomes (Sullivan, 1982). It is, therefore, not yet possible to say whether the successful outcomes are uniquely due to the process of nursing care. The data available about patient satisfaction with nurse practitioner care are encouraging, and suggest that the role in primary care is acceptable to most people.

Acknowledgement

The author wishes to thank Dr S Greenfield for her invaluable contribution to the design, administration and analysis of the patients' questionnaire. Dr Greenfield does not have joint authorship as the conclusion and interpretation are solely the views of the author.

References

Anderson E R (1973) The Role of the Nurse. London: Royal College of Nursing.
Chen S C, Barkauskas V H & Chen E (1984) Health problems encountered by nurse practitioners and physicians in general medical clinics. Research in Nursing and Health, 7, 79–86
Cartwright A & Anderson R (1981) General Practice Revisited. London: Tavistock Publications
Eisenberg L (1977) The search for care. In Knowles J (ed) Doing Better and Feeling Worse: Health in the United States. New York: W W Norton
Gray J (1982) The effect of a doctor's sex on the doctor–patient relationship. Journal of the Royal College of General Practitioners, 32, 167–169
Hull F M & Hull F S (1984) Time and the general practitioner: the patient's view. Journal of the Royal College of General Practitioners, 34, 71–75
Hogan K A & Hogan R A (1982) Assessment of the consumer's potential response to the nurse practitioner model. Journal of Nursing Education, 21, 4–12
Kenkre J, Drury V W M & Lancashire R J (1985) Nurse management of hypertension clinics in general practice assisted by a computer. Family Practice, 2, 17–22
Levine J I, Orr S T, Sheatsley D W et al (1978) The nurse practitioner: role, physician utilisation, patient acceptance. Nursing Research, 27, 245–253
Lewis C & Resnick B (1967) Nurse clinics and progressive ambulatory care. New England Journal of Medicine, 277, 1236–1241
Oakley A (1984) The importance of being a nurse, Nursing Times, 80, 24–27
Ramsay J, McKenzie J & Fish D (1982) Physicians and nurse practitioners; do they provide

equal health care? *American Journal of Public Health*, **72**, 55–57.

Reedy B L (1972) The general practice nurse. *Update*, **5**, 75–78

Sullivan J (1982) Research on nurse practitioners: process behind the outcome? *American Journal of Public Health*, **72**, 8–9

Watkins L & Wagner E (1982) Nurse practitioner and physician adherence to standing orders: criteria for consultation or referral. *American Journal fo Public Health*, **72**, 55–57

11
Where Next? Concluding Comments

BARBARA STILWELL   ANN BOWLING

One major conclusion to emerge from this volume is that the roles of practice nurse and nurse practitioner involve a major degree of overlap.

Although there is no formally recognised nurse practitioner role in the UK a significant minority of practice nurses feel they are extending their roles in this direction. The programme in Oxford to develop systematic cardiovascular risk screening programmmes heavily involving practice nurses, has given further impetus to the actual development of a more autonomous and advanced nursing role. Whatever it is called – nurse practitioners or family nurse practitioner – there is clearly a place for this role within primary care in the UK, particularly if any attempt is to be made to realise the World Health Organization's objectives of Health for All by the Year 2000 (World Health Organization, 1985). With the UKCC's proposals to redesign basic nurse training, with facilities for post-basic specialist courses, the way is being paved for the development of a nationally agreed and recognised practice nurse course. It is likely, in view of the Royal College of Nursing's guidelines on the subject, that this training will prepare them for an extended technical, preventive and (limited) diagnostic role. Thus it is even more important to define clearly the difference between the role of the practice nurse and that of the nurse practitioner.

It seems to us that the role of a nurse practitioner is not defined solely by the range of tasks performed nor by skill in diagnosis or treatment. Rather, the role encompasses these skills, but represents too a philosophy of autonomous nursing practice, together with accountability for that practice. Consider the following styles of care given by two imaginary nurses.

Nurse A has been a nurse in general practice for ten years. Patients are free to see her when they wish to, and choose to do so mainly for ear syringing, minor injuries or immunisations. Nurse A is an excellent nurse, competent, efficient and caring. When a patient consults her to have an injection, for example, she knows exactly what she requires because the information will be in the patient's notes (she insists on that) and gives the injection speedily and painlessly. When checking that the injection is written in the notes, Nurse A sometimes notices that a patient's blood pressure has not been checked. She also notices other risk factors, like smoking or obesity, and will always give patients appropriate leaflets. Nurse A is popular with the doctors in her practice, who regard her as a first-rate worker. She does not go to their clinical meetings because she has not been invited and, anyway, would probably not wish to.

Nurse B has been a practice nurse for seven years. Patients are free to consult her whenever they wish, and, as with Nurse A, the majority of patients will come to her for minor injuries, complaints and ear syringing. When a patient comes for an injection, Nurse B does not immediately give the medication, but first asks him/her what injection he/she is to have, and whether or not he/she has had one before. Then Nurse B asks about any side-effects the person has had, or may have, from the injection. (Nurse B will have checked this information in the notes beforehand.) If the injection is medicinal (e.g. for rheumatoid arthritis or anaemia), Nurse B asks how the patient is coping with the condition. Does she manage her job/shopping/housework? How is her family? Before giving the injection, Nurse B checks the patient's notes: she, too, assesses risk factors and also links them with the present condition. She talks to the patient about any screening that seems necessary and arranges for a return visit for a longer appointment, when she will have time to help him/her set long-term goals to improve his/her health status. At the practice clinical meetings, Nurse B usually has a contribution to make to discussions of particular or general disease management, because her nursing care is concerned with unique aspects of patient care. Sometimes the doctors question Nurse B about the advice she has given patients, and she is prepared to accept criticism, as well as praise, on occasion. Sometimes, the doctors ask Nurse B for advice too.

The differences between these two styles of care are subtle, and yet important. A nurse practitioner is practising *nursing*, not being an assistant to the physician. It was shown in Chapter 1 that American nurse practitioners have not found it easy, at times, to work on an equal basis as an equal colleague with physicians, yet collaborative practice is important for patients and may, in the end, be more satisfying for nurses and doctors.

The findings of Greenfield *et al* (1987) and of Cater and Hawthorn (Chapter 9), that not all practice nurses wish to extend their roles, indicate that the roles of practice nurse and nurse practitioner can be divided. However, this must be done with great care, and after consultation with representatives of practice nurses themselves, in order to avoid role overlap and conflict and potential feelings of frustration and job dissatisfaction in the future. There is a danger of the latter if practice nurses are left with only technical tasks to perform.

The evidence indicates that the political climate in primary health care is ripe for experimentation with nurse roles. The methods for promoting the extended role of the nurse and of overcoming any remaining resistance to change have been outlined in this volume – thus there is little excuse if the nurse practitioner role in the UK fails to develop alongside that of the practice nurse.

In 1985 the World Health Organization suggested that if we are to achieve the goal of Health for All by the Year 2000 nurses must lead the way. We have shown in this volume that nursing has an undeveloped potential to improve the health status of the chronically sick, the elderly and, by anticipatory care, the well of all ages. The World Health Organization (1985) implied that nursing could act as a powerhouse for change, and in doing so would receive their full support. The challenge is there; it remains to be seen if it will be taken up.

References

Greenfield S, Stilwell B & Drury M (1987) Practice nurses: social and occupational characteristics. *Journal of the Royal College of General Practitioners*, **37**, 341–345
World Health Organization (1985) *Targets for Health for All by the Year 2000*. Copenhagen: World Health Organization, Regional Office for Europe

Index